It's the Economy, Friends

Understanding the Growth Dilemma

Quaker Institute for the Future Pamphlet Series

Quaker Institute for the Future Pamphlets aim to provide critical information and understanding born of careful discernment on social, economic, and ecological realities, inspired by the testimonies and values of the Religious Society of Friends (Quakers). We live in a time when social and ecological issues are converging toward catastrophic breakdown. Human adaptation to social, economic and planetary realities must be re-thought and re-designed. *Quaker Institute for the Future Pamphlets* are dedicated to this calling based on a spiritual and ethical commitment to "right relationship" with Earth's whole commonwealth of life.

Quaker Institute for the Future

It's the Economy, Friends
Understanding the Growth Dilemma

Edited by
Ed Dreby
Keith Helmuth
Margaret Mansfield

Quaker Institute for the Future Pamphlet 5
Quaker Institute for the Future 2012

Published for Quaker Institute for the Future by *Producciones de la Hamaca*, Caye Caulker, Belize <producciones-hamaca.com>

ISBN: 978-976-8142-43-6

It's the Economy, Friends is the fifth in a series of Quaker Institute for the Future Pamphlets:

Series ISBN: 978-976-8142-21-4

Producciones de la Hamaca is dedicated to:

—Celebration and documentation of Earth
      and all her inhabitants,
—Restoration and conservation of Earth's
      natural resources,
—Creative expression of the sacredness of
      Earth and Spirit.

Table of Contents

v

Preface

In times of crisis, profound questions sometimes emerge in straight-forward and clarifying ways. With the world's dominant economic system now struggling to recover from near collapse, it seems important to ask: "What is the economy for?"

The conventional answer, that the economy is for ever increasing material wealth through unlimited economic growth, is no longer coherent, either for societal or ecosystem well-being. Quaker Institute for the Future (QIF) examined this question in *Right Relationship: Building a Whole Earth Economy*, and concluded that "the purpose of the economy is to preserve and enhance the integrity, resilience and beauty of the whole commonwealth of life."[1]

Since 2009 Philadelphia Yearly Meeting (PYM) of the Religious Society of Friends (Quakers) has also been examining this question through the lens of "right relationship" and in 2010 concluded:

> We believe that by any religious, moral, or ethical standard, our economy should serve all our people, the children who come after us, and the commonwealth of life on which our existence depends. ...

> Let us seek and speak truth about the failures of our current system more openly and boldly ... to learn what is needed, and to use what we learn to bring our economy into right relationship with the ideals of our history, the welfare of our posterity, and the well-being of our only earth.

This QIF Pamphlet (QIF #5) is in collaboration with the Growth Dilemma Project of PYM. Our title comes from David Ciscel, a Quaker, an economist, and Professor Emeritus, University of Memphis.[2] He altered the famous slogan used in the 1992 Clinton presidential campaign, "It's the economy, stupid!" By replacing "stupid" with "Friends," David Ciscel signals a different approach to a subject fraught with conflict. We've chosen this title in part for its thoughtful ambiguity. For us, Ciscel strikes a note which points not only toward the Quaker community, but also toward the manner and tone we think essential for a wider public dialogue about the failures of the current economic system.

The Growth Dilemma Project website states that "humanity faces a profound dilemma. The economies of virtually all nations require growth to function. Yet more growth makes the wealthiest even wealthier, while unemployment, hunger, and violence are widespread, and human economies are already larger than Earth's ecosystems can continue to support."

Philadelphia Yearly Meeting has approved a set of core principles that reflect this truth and are rooted in values we share with many of our sisters and brothers from other faith traditions. PYM has charged the Growth Dilemma Project to promote a Quaker witness on ecology and the economy. While Friends may be in broad agreement about the values we should promote and the problems that must be addressed, we do not agree on what causes these problems, or what should be done about them.

Some Friends think that with sufficient political will and wisdom, and with a strategic adjustment of incentives, the existing economic model can enable society to shift from its environmentally destructive trajectory to an ecologically sound mode of adaptation. They are convinced that "good" economic growth is essential to meet humanity's needs, and to build an ecologically sustainable economy.

Others Friends are convinced that the current system makes economic growth inseparable from increased material and energy consumption. They think an alternative system must be devised so a society can prosper as its economy's demand for physical resources is brought within Earth's bio-productive capacity. This will require overdeveloped regions to use substantially fewer resources so poorer regions can develop and use the resources they need for a decent and dignified way of life.

It's the Economy, Friends (QIF #5) contains a series of essays by different authors organized into three chapters designed to provide: 1) a context for examining these issues based upon a history of Quaker witness, 2) a description of basic economic concepts from both orthodox and ecological perspectives, and 3) reflections on ethics, ecology, and economics. While this pamphlet was written for Friends, we hope it will be useful to the general reader, who might want to skip the Quaker history and begin with Chapter 2.

The forthcoming companion volume, *Confronting the Growth Dilemma* (QIF pamphlet #6), will focus on two contrasting views about our current economic system with respect to the social and ecological problems it is failing to address. It will also describe a number of recommendations for altering the current system to help create an economy that works well for humanity and for the whole of life.

Beginning in 2003, many Friends helped create the material that makes up these two pamphlets. We especially want to thank Kim Carlyle, Gary Lapreziosa, David Ciscel, Pamela Haines, Walter Haines, David Ross, Don Kesselheim, and Hollister Knowlton. We remember Barbara Hirshkowitz for her editorial consulting.

Much of the material in this pamphlet has been adapted from a three-volume study guide, *Seeds of Violence, Seeds of Hope,* published from 2005 to 2007 by Friends Testimonies and Economics, a project of PYM and Quaker Earthcare Witness.[3] George Lakey, Stephen Loughlin, and Ed Snyder provided new essays for which we are grateful. We thank Herman Daly for permission to publish his essay "Boundless Bull," and Elise Boulding for permission to reprint two of Kenneth Boulding's essays.

The Growth Dilemma Project Group and participants in its monthly Gatherings for Discussion and Discernment have provided encouragement and support all along the way. Judy Lumb and Barbara Day prepared the final manuscript in a way that greatly improved its clarity and quality. We are most grateful for the dedication with which they applied their editing skills to this project.

We intend *It's the Economy, Friends* to help general readers have a broader and deeper understanding of the dilemmas that our society faces about our current growth economy. We hope it will be appropriate for workshop and study-group use, and that it will prompt readers to continue with its companion volume, QIF Pamphlet #6 *Confronting the Growth Dilemma.*

Ed Dreby and Margaret Mansfield, Mt. Holly NJ, U.S.

Keith Helmuth, Woodstock NB, Canada

May 2012

CHAPTER ONE
Toward a Witness on Ecology and the Economy
Keith Helmuth and Ed Dreby

As we take aim at understanding the economy in an ecological context, the moral dimensions of our heritage of Quaker faith and practice reflect both a long tradition and a recent convergence of concerns about economics, ecology, and ethics within the Religious Society of Friends.

Early Quaker History

From early Quaker history, three figures stand out for their translation of religious values into action on economics and human betterment: John Bellers, William Penn, and John Woolman.

John Bellers (1654–1725)[1] was a successful London cloth merchant who turned his attention to the study of society and economy in a way unprecedented for his time. When Karl Marx discovered his writing, he acknowledged Bellers' importance in the history of political economy. In concert with his Quaker faith and values, something began working within Bellers that drew his talents and energy into a kind of systems analysis that had little in the way of antecedents. He manifested a new way of thinking about the connections between social structures, societal problems, and economics.

As a result of his observations and analysis, and his concern for the plight of the poor, he conceived of a completely new institution, a planned and managed enterprise that included agricultural production, manufacturing shops, housing, healthcare, and education for both children and adults. He envisioned a highly self-provisioning cooperative community in which the poor could gain both a living and an education, and investors could earn a profit. He prepared a detailed proposal, complete with calculations of investment, expenses, production, and income from the sale of products, and he tried to convince both private investors and government to support a pilot project.

1

Although he never succeeded in assembling the investment needed, his work was a key influence on Robert Owen 150 years later when he established "Villages of Cooperation" at New Lanark with Quaker financial support. Owen's realization of Beller's vision is particularly significant because it led to the Cooperative Movement that has since enabled many people world-wide to improve their economic and social conditions.

William Penn (1644-1718)[5] is the best-known Quaker figure in history, and for good reason. He founded the Quaker colony of Pennsylvania and provided a template of democracy that shaped political and social development in the United States and elsewhere. William Penn was a close friend of John Bellers, so they may have influenced each other in their approaches to social, economic, political, and human development issues. The origins of town planning and the integration of human settlements with environmentally conscious stewardship can be seen in Penn's innovative approach to the carefully planned layout for the development of Philadelphia.

John Woolman (1720-1772)[6] is best known for prompting the movement among Quakers for the abolition of slavery, but he also paid careful attention to a whole range of factors and relationships that made up the colonial economy of the Delaware Valley region of his time. He wrote a number of essays that distill his observations and analysis of economic life with a surprisingly astute ecological perspective. His *Journal*, pamphlets, and essays record a deep concern for the suffering, oppression, and spiritual disorders attending the social and economic life of his time.

One of the remarkable characteristics of John Woolman's discernment is that virtually all his perceptions about spiritual disorders cross over into their social and economic consequences, and all his discussions of social and economic disorders cross over into their spiritual consequences. Woolman had an intuitive understanding of "right relationship" with regard to the land, the use and care of animals, and the larger questions of human settlement and adaptation. He understood the ecological integrity of Creation and saw the disruption and degradation that occur when the dominion of privilege and wealth accumulation drive human settlement and land use.

In 1763 Woolman's concern for the aboriginal peoples of the region led him to make a journey to what is now north-central Pennsylvania to visit two of their village settlements. His *Journal* contains a diary of the trip. On the 13th day the 6th month he writes:

The sun appearing, we set forward, and as I rode over the barren hills my Meditations were on the alterations of the circumstances of the natives of this land since the coming in of the English. The lands near the sea are conveniently situated for fishing. The lands near the rivers where the tides flow, and some above, are in many places fertile and not mountainous, while the running of the tides makes passing up and down easy with any kind of traffic. Those natives have in some places, for trifling considerations, sold their inheritance so favourably situated, and in other places have been driven back by superior force, so that in many places ... [they] have to pass over mountains, swamps and barren deserts, where travel is very troublesome, in bringing their skins and furs to trade with us. By the extending of English settlements and partly by English hunters, those wild beasts they chiefly depend on for a subsistence are not as plentiful as they were. ...

My own will and desires being now very much broken and my heart with much earnestness turned to the Lord, to whom alone I looked for help in the dangers before me, I had the prospect of the English along the coast for upward of nine hundred miles where I have traveled. And the favourable situation of the English and the difficulties attending the natives in many places, and the Negroes, were open before me. And a weighty and heavenly care came over my mind, and love filled my heart toward all mankind, in which I felt a strong engagement that we might be obedient to the Lord while in tender mercies he is yet calling to us, and so attend to pure universal righteousness. ...

And in this lonely journey I did this day greatly bewail the spreading of a wrong spirit, believing that the prosperous, convenient situation of the English requires a constant attention to divine love and wisdom, to guide and support us in a way answerable to the will of the good gracious, and almighty Being who hath an equal regard to all mankind. And here luxury and covetousness, and numerous oppressions and other evils attending them, appeared very afflicting to me, and I felt in that which is immutable that the seeds of great calamity and desolation are sown and growing fast on this continent. Nor have I words sufficient to set forth that longing I then felt that we who are placed along the coast, and have tasted the love and goodness of God, might arise in his strength and like faithful messengers labour to check the growth of these seeds, that they may not ripen to the ruin of our posterity.[7]

Today, instead of picturing just nine hundred miles of the North American Mid-Atlantic coast and a hundred miles or so inland, we must picture the whole continent, indeed, the whole earth. We must picture the relationships between wealth and poverty, and between land, resources, and human settlements everywhere. Woolman understood that, in right ordering, the financial system depends on the production system, which, in turn, depends on the sustainability of earth's ecosystem. He saw the tendency in the economic behavior of his time to have these fundamental dependencies exactly the wrong way round: the financial system driving the production system, and the production system impacting ecosystems without regard for their integrity or sustainability. Woolman writes:

> Wealth desired for its own sake obstructs the increase of virtue, and large possessions in the hands of selfish men have a bad tendency, for by their means too small a number of people are employed in things useful; and therefore they, or some of them, are necessitated to labour too hard, while others would want business to earn their bread were not employment's invented which, having no real use, serving only to please the vain mind.

> Rents set on lands are often so high that persons who have but small substance are straightened in hiring a plantation; and while tenants are healthy and prosperous in business, they often find occasion to labour harder than was intended by our gracious Creator. Oxen and horses are often seen to work when, through heat and too much labour, their eyes and the emotion of their bodies manifest that they are oppressed. ... Many poor people are so thronged in their business that it is difficult for them to provide shelter suitable for their animals in great storms.[8]

> If interest were lower, grain lower and kept more plentiful in our Country, wages of hired men might with reason be lower also. Hence encouragement would naturally arise to husbandmen, to raise more Sheep and flax, and prepare means to employ many more poor people amongst us.

> The high interest on money which lieth on many husbandmen is often a means of their struggling for present profit. ... I have known landholders who paid interest for large sums of money, and being intent on paying their debts by raising grain and by sending abroad great quantities of grain, ... have by too much tilling, so robbed the earth of its natural fatness, that the produce thereof hath grown light ... and the fatness of our land diminished.[9]

While Woolman was observing and analyzing the agricultural and commercial economy of his time, his perception of right and wrong

4

relationships in both the social economy and in the economy of earth's ecosystems was prescient. His intuition and systems-thinking forecast the rise of ecological understanding and the discipline of ecological economics. In addition to the advance in moral intuition and reasoning that Woolman's Quaker ethos brought to the issue of slavery, he also opened a window on the ethics of right relationship in economics and in the human use of earth's ecosystems. The luminous vision of right relationship that Woolman drew from his Quaker heritage is now the ethical companion of the science of ecosystem integrity, and the grounding of our ecological understanding of the human-earth relationship.

18th and 19th Century Quaker Witness

Bellers, Penn, and Woolman manifested the inclination to integrate: to see connections among seemingly disparate domains of experience and social reality. This inclination naturally arises in the Quaker form of silent, waiting worship, and is central to the Quaker testimony on integrity. Yet, often, when Friends are led to a concern, and led to do something about it, the focus tends to be on a particular manifestation of a problem situation, rather than on the origin of the problem itself.

In the 18th and 19th centuries this was largely the case with Quaker activism, whether it was about education reform, hospital care, prison improvement, women's rights, slavery, or the plight of Native Americans having been dispossessed of their homelands. John Woolman wrote about the systemic nature of slavery, yet the efforts to do something about it were, at first, didactic: free your slaves, end the slave trade, help the runaways. The movement to abolish the institution of slavery and make it illegal became a systemic approach for that particular oppression, but the wider question of the exploitation of labor to advance the accumulation of great wealth remained largely unaddressed. John Bellers summed up this wider system of oppression and inequity with an aphorism; "The Labours of the poor are the mines of the rich."

The end of slavery did not touch this wider exploitation of labor, and the oppression of African Americans continued by virtue of the racism that structured employment opportunities. The system of overall economic oppression of workers, land, and animals, that Woolman repeatedly addressed, continued unabated.

After the American Civil War, as industrialization proceeded, concerns about the capitalist economy's oppressive exploitation of workers came to the fore. At the same time, there were many successful Quaker industrialists and entrepreneurs whose values rejected the oppression of workers for higher profit, and were scrupulous in treating their employees with great fairness, unusual dignity, and close attention to family needs. This witness for fairness and equity was especially notable in the old joke that Quakers "came to do good and ended up doing very well." This concern about the ethics of the economy continued to develop among Friends in the 20th century.

20th Century Quaker Witness

In 1916 London Yearly Meeting held a Conference on War and Social Order and published an eight-point document titled "Foundations of a True Social Order." The first two points articulate the religious and ethical foundations of Quaker values and the remaining six points deal with economic fairness and social justice. [10]

In 1934, in the midst of the Great Depression, three Quakers, serving as the Social Economics Committee of the Industrial Relations Section of Friends General Conference, presented a report to the Annual Session entitled, "A Statement of Economic Objectives."[11] This remarkable report takes up the full scope of the circumstances of the Depression, providing a systematic analysis and an integrated set of remedial actions for ending the economic and social catastrophe. They called on Friends to seriously study the economic crisis and act toward its resolution. This was not strange for Friends at the time as some Quakers were deeply involved in Roosevelt's New Deal.

In 1965, New York Yearly Meeting founded Friends World College (FWC),[12] which, under the direction of Morris Mitchell, established five study centers around the world. The curriculum was based on the direct study of world problems, such as, poverty, racism, and environmental degradation, and their emerging solutions. FWC pioneered studying abroad by taking the world as its campus. The program continues as Global College of Long Island University.

Four 20th century Friends are notable for their contributions at the intersection of economics, ecology, and social justice, and for the way this holistic concern has informed their professional and civic engagements: Gilbert White, Elizabeth Watson, Ursula Franklin, and Kenneth Boulding. Only recently has their work made influential contributions to an emerging Quaker concern about ecology and the economy.

Gilbert White (1911-2006)[13] was prominent in geographic, environmental, and human ecology research, and in international water management. In government, college administration, Quaker organizations, and in international watershed negotiations and conflict resolution, he was noted for his leadership in the kind of collaborative discernment and decision-making that is characteristic of Quakerism at its best. He was a pioneering figure in understanding and articulating the ecological basis of resilient human settlement and appropriate economic development.

Elizabeth Watson (1914-2006)[14] was perhaps best known as a frequent speaker at Quaker gatherings, workshops and conferences. Her influence rested strongly on her personal presence at these events as well as on her thoughtful writing. Her book, *Guests of My Life* (1979), recounts how, in a time of great loss, she finds healing in the works of several poets and a novelist who express a rootedness in Earth and in the fullness of its encompassing and nurturing reality. She showed how a deep identification with Earth's commonwealth of life and a passion for social justice emerges from great literature. In her last work, *Healing Ourselves and Our Earth,* she gathered her study of theology, literature, feminism, and ecology into a ringing call to transform the human-Earth relationship and the social, economic and political behavior that now endangers the future of humanity.

Ursula Franklin (1921-)[15] has long been active in the peace and justice work of the Quaker community in Canada. From her position as a professor of physics and materials science at the University of Toronto, she has been active at the highest levels of science, technology, and industry, both in Canadian society and internationally. In 1989 she presented a series of lectures on the Canadian Broadcasting Corporation that was developed into the book, *The Real World of Technology,* which has become a widely cited reference on understanding the relationships between technology, economics, and society. In the 1999 edition she places great emphasis on the environmental context: "Yet if sane and healthy communities are to prevail, much more weight has to be placed on maintaining the non-negotiable ties of all people to the biosphere."[16]

Kenneth Boulding (1910-1993)[17] grounded his professional work in the quest for human betterment that Friends have advanced since the origins of Quakerism. Boulding is best known to Quakers as the author of *The Naylor Sonnets* and as a proponent of peace research studies. In the wider society, however, he was a prominent economist. He was among the first in his field to call attention to the failure of modern economic thought to address the need of adapting to an Earth that had suddenly become much smaller and more fragile, relative to the human population it supports.

Kenneth Boulding was not an ecologist and he was a strong advocate for the benefits of markets. But the issues he raised reflected an ecological perspective: the encroachment of humans on the habitats of other species, the need to find substitutes for non-renewable resources without exceeding the sustainable yield of renewable resources, and the possibility that human wastes would exceed Earth's capacities to absorb them. He also identified these as systemic problems in which our economic institutions have a central role.

Earth as a Spaceship

"Earth as a Spaceship,"[18] was presented by Kenneth Boulding (1910-1993) to a meeting of the Washington State University Committee on Space Sciences, May 10, 1965. It has become a classic statement that sets the stage for understanding economic activity within the reality of Earth's ecological context.

In the imagination of those who are sensitive to the realities of our era, the earth has become a space ship, and this, perhaps, is the most important single fact of our day. For millennia, the earth in men's minds was flat and illimitable. Today, as a result of exploration, speed, and the explosion of scientific knowledge, earth has become a tiny sphere, closed, limited, crowded, and hurtling through space to unknown destinations. This change in man's image of his home affects his behavior in many ways, and is likely to affect it much more in the future.

It is not only that man's image of the earth has changed; the reality of the world social system has changed. As long as man was small in numbers and limited in technology, he could realistically regard the earth as an infinite reservoir, an infinite source of inputs and an infinite cesspool for outputs. Today we can no longer make this assumption. Earth has become a space ship, not only in our imagination but also in the hard realities of the social, biological, and physical system in which man is enmeshed. In what we might call the "old days," when man was small in numbers and earth was large, he could pollute it with impunity, though even then he frequently destroyed his immediate environment and had to move on to a new spot, which he then proceeded to destroy. Now man can no longer do this; he must live in the whole system, in which he must recycle his wastes and really face up to the problem of the increase in material entropy which his activities create. In a space ship there are no sewers.

Let me suggest, then, some of the consequences of earth becoming a space ship. In the first place, it is absolutely necessary for man now to develop a technology that is different from the one on which he now bases his high-level societies. High-level societies are now based on the consumption of fossil fuels and ores, none of which, at present rates of consumption, are likely to last more than a few hundred years. A stable, circular-flow high-level technology is conceivable in which we devote inputs of energy to the concentration of materials into useful form, sufficient to compensate for the diffusion of materials which takes place in their use. At the moment we take fuels and burn them, we take concentrated deposits of iron ore for instance, and phosphates, and we spread these throughout the world in dumps, and we flush them out to the oceans in sewers. The stable high-level technology will have to rely on the oceans and the atmosphere as a basic resource from which materials may be concentrated in sufficient quantity to overcome their diffusion through consumption. Even this, of course, will require constant inputs of energy. There is no way for the closed system to prevent the increase of entropy. Earth, fortunately, has a constant input of energy from the sun, and by the time that goes, man will probably have abandoned earth; and we have also the possibility of almost unlimited energy inputs from nuclear fusion, if we can find means of harnessing it usefully.

Man is finally going to have to face the fact that he is a biological system living in an ecological system, and that his survival power is going to depend on his developing symbiotic relationships of a closed-cycle character with all the other elements and populations of the world of ecological systems. What this means, in effect, is that all the other forms of life will have to be domesticated, even if on wildlife preserves.

The consequences of earth becoming a space ship for the social system are profound and little understood. It is clear that much human behavior and many human institutions in the past, which were appropriate to an infinite earth, are entirely inappropriate to a small closed space ship. We cannot have cowboys and Indians, for instance, in a space ship, or even a cowboy ethic. We cannot afford

9

unrestrained conflict, and we almost certainly cannot afford national sovereignty in an unrestricted sense. On the other hand, we must beware of pushing the analogy too far. In a small ship, there would almost have to be a dictatorial political system with a captain, and a planned economy. A voyaging space ship, like a battleship, almost has to be a centrally planned economy. A large space ship with three billion passengers, however, or perhaps ten billion, may have a very different social structure. Large social organizations are very different from small. It may be able to have much more individual freedom, a price system and a market economy of a limited and controlled kind, and even democratic political institutions. There must be, however, cybernetic or homeostatic mechanisms for preventing the overall variables of the social system from going beyond a certain range. There must, for instance, be machinery for controlling the total numbers of the population; there must be machinery for controlling conflict processes and for preventing perverse social dynamic processes of escalation and inflation. One of the major problems of social science is how to devise institutions which will combine this overall homeostatic control with individual freedom and mobility. I believe this problem to be not insoluble, though not yet solved.

Once we begin to look at earth as a space ship, the appalling extent of our ignorance about it is almost frightening. This is true of the level of every science. We know practically nothing, for instance, about the long-run dynamics even of the physical system of the earth. We do not understand, for instance, the machinery of ice ages, the real nature of geological stability or disturbance, the incidence of volcanism and earthquakes, and we understand fantastically little about that enormously complex heat engine known as the atmosphere. ...

The moral of all this is that man must be made to realize that all his major problems are still unsolved, and that a very large and massive intellectual effort is still necessary to solve them. In the meantime we are wasting our intellectual resources on insoluble problems like unilateral national defense and on low-priority achievements like putting a man on the moon. This is no way to run a space ship.

10

Excerpts from *"The Economics of the Coming Spaceship Earth"*

In 1966 Kenneth Boulding presented "The Economics of the Coming Spaceship Earth" at the Sixth Resources for the Future Forum in Washington, D.C.[19] The excerpts included here sharpen the scope of the fundamental transition in human economic behavior that will be required for sustainable adaptation to our planetary circumstances.

We are now in the middle of a long process of transition in the image which man has had of himself and his environment. Primitive man, and to a large extent also men of the early civilizations, imagined themselves to be living on a virtually illimitable plane. There was almost always somewhere beyond the known limits of human habitation, and over a very large part of the time that man has been on earth, there has always been something like a frontier. That is, there was always some place else to go when things get too difficult, either by reason of the deterioration of the natural environment or the social structure in places where people happened to live. The image of the frontier is probably one of the oldest images of mankind, and it is not surprising that we find it hard to get rid of. ….

The closed earth of the future requires economic principles which are somewhat different from those of the open earth of the past. ….

For the sake of picturesqueness, I am tempted to call the open economy the "cowboy economy," the cowboy being symbolic of the illimitable plains and also associated with reckless, exploitative, romantic, and violent behavior, which is characteristic of open societies. The closed economy of the future might similarly be called the "spaceman economy," in which the earth has become a single spaceship, without unlimited resources of anything, either for extraction or pollution, and in which, therefore, man must find his place in a cyclical ecological system which is capable of continuous reproduction of material form even though it cannot escape having inputs of energy.

The difference between the two types of economies becomes apparent in the attitudes toward consumption. In the cowboy economy, consumption is regarded as a good thing, and production likewise; and the success of the economy is measured by the amount of throughput from the "factors of production," a part of which, at any rate, is extracted from the reservoirs of raw materials

11

and non-economic objects, and another part of which is output into the reservoirs of pollution. ... By contrast, in the spaceman economy, throughput is by no means a desideratum, and is indeed to be regarded as something to be minimized rather than maximized.

In the spaceman economy, what we are primarily concerned with is stock maintenance, and any technological change which results in the maintenance of a given stock with lessened throughput (that is, less production and consumption) is clearly a gain. This idea that both production and consumption are bad things rather than good things is very strange to economists, who have been obsessed with income flow concepts to the exclusion, almost, of capital stock concepts. ....

Friends Committee on National Legislation (FCNL)[20] published "Goals for a Just Society, Jobs, and Assured Income in 1969."[21] This document is a Quaker landmark, a coherent and cogent synthesis of moral reasoning and policy proposals for a better human future. FCNL also initiated the work of Sam and Miriam Levering that led to the UN Law of the Sea Treaty in 1982.[22]

The care of the environment as a religious issue emerged in the World Council of Churches in the 1980s as a call to restore the "Integrity of Creation." In 1987, at Friends General Conference Gathering, a small group of Friends was led to make care of the Earth a spiritual witness. They established Friends Committee on Unity with Nature, later renamed Quaker Earthcare Witness (QEW).[23] QEW has provided a steady flow of educational material on the spiritual basis for Earthcare and practical advice for ecologically sound living. In 1997, Britain Yearly Meeting published its "Corporate Social Testimony,"[24] on what is happening at the intersection of the economy, environment, and social equity.

The systemic problems of modern industrial societies that Boulding described 45 years ago have yet to be recognized or addressed by those who wield power and influence. Even though more is now known about human impacts on global and regional ecosystems, little has been done to significantly reorient industrial societies' economic policies or institutions. The changes since then have intensified these impacts. The work of Friends continues.

21st Century Quaker Witness

At the turn of the 21st century, many Friends in the United States and Canada were involved with Earthcare concerns through the conservation and environmental movements. Yet this calling to work for the well-being of the Earth tended to be individual. The Society of Friends as a whole was focused on peace and equality issues only as they affect human beings.

Ecological Integrity and Religious Faith

This essay was written by Keith Helmuth for the 2001 Session of Philadelphia Yearly Meeting of the Religious Society of Friends and published in Friends Journal in August 2001.

There is a growing recognition that the state of Earth's ecological integrity is not just one more concern to be added to an already long list of concerns. There is a growing sense that to continue representing the ecological issue in our corporate forums as a "special interest" is to remain unresponsive to a central spiritual task of our time: readapting human settlement and economic behavior to the biotic integrity of Earth. The ecological situation is not a concern in the usual sense of the word, nor is it a special interest. It is the foundation of all concerns and the most general and comprehensive interest possible. It is both the given and created context out of which everything we care about and work for develops. The human-Earth relationship is the context in which all concerns are situated. Justice, equity, peace and spiritual well-being have no other home than the human-Earth relationship in which to flourish or wither, as the case may be.

All the areas of human concern that Friends have traditionally addressed will be negatively affected by the ongoing, disruptive impact of human activity on biospheric integrity. Ethnic, political, and economic violence will be exacerbated. Human settlement, livelihood, and food production will increasingly be disrupted. Social and economic inequities will be magnified. Deficiency, stress, trauma, and disability disorders will multiply. Spiritual disorientation will spread.

All of these phenomena are already on the increase. Continued deterioration of Earth's habitability will drive them all into more and more extreme forms. Given the Quaker heritage of bonding religious faith into the work of human betterment, it is difficult to see how we can avoid bringing this crisis in the human-Earth relationship into the center of our perspective.

In 1990 the World Council of Churches held a ten-day convocation in Seoul, South Korea on Justice, Peace, and the Integrity of Creation. This convocation identified the ecological disruption that will attend the advance of global warming as the preeminent threat to Earth's communities of life. It further agreed that because human economic activity is contributing to global warming, this situation is an issue of fundamental import that must be addressed by the world's communities of faith. A decade later the global warming issue is front and center on the witness and action agendas of many religious groups and associations.

Although the human patterns of ecological violation are manifold, the specter of ecological disruption that will accompany the advance of global warming rises like a particularly ominous thunderhead over the landscapes and shorelines of Earth. Human-induced, disruptive climate change epitomizes what is wrong with the current human-Earth relationship. It is an incontrovertible fact that every day human economic activity is damaging and destroying Earth's ability to support the commonwealth of life. For those who have come into a full realization of this situation, the problem verges on the unbearable. It has a mind-numbing and spirit-damaging quality.

It is difficult to see how we can claim a clear sense of Divine presence while all around us the channels of energy on which we depend, and the patterns of economic activity that support us, are steadily grinding down and functionally disabling the integrity of Creation. It is not just a matter of Earth's environment becoming an increasingly less hospitable place. It is also a matter of increasingly losing the sense of the Divine as a whole Earth reality, as a cosmic loom interweaving all communities of life. The evidence of this cultural devolution is all around us. We cannot go on disrupting, breaking up, and laying waste the functional relationships that compose the integrity of Creation and expect to retain a viable sense of the Divine.

As ecological disruption develops, the issues of human adaptation will become increasingly skewed toward the struggle for bare survival on the one hand, and the struggle to defend wealth and access to the means of life on the other. This is already the situation we are in. As hardedge survival and the protection of privilege become the dominant factors of social existence, it will

14

become ever more difficult to bring ecological consciousness to bear on public policy. Nothing less than the ability to maintain an overarching faith, an encompassing sense of the Divine, and to work with conviction for the common good are now at stake in the unraveling of the human-Earth relationship.

If our faith is seeking a mode of expression and breadth of address in the world that reaches to the center of the human dilemma, it must move fully into the ecological worldview. This perspective will provide clear and useful openings at a fundamental level into all peace, justice, and equity issues and enable us to help reconceive the whole project of human adaptation to the environments of Earth.

With the imperative of ecologically sustainable adaptation firmly lodged at the center of our faith, we can then develop our work for peace, justice, and equity in ways that contribute as fully as possible to a reweaving of the human-Earth relationship. Thus we can keep alive an encompassing and nurturing sense of the Divine. Even if we do not succeed in moving our society onto a sustainable path, at least we will know that we have done the right thing. That may be small comfort, but it may also be the difference between a sense of faithfulness and the despair that will certainly overtake denial and inaction.

We have now come to the time when the options are perfectly clear: either we continue down the road of unlimited economic expansion and increasing energy use until a convergence of ecological breakdowns stops our cultural momentum, or we place ecologically sustainable adaptation at the leading edge of human settlement and economic behavior.

This dilemma and this choice bear a striking resemblance to the issue of slaveholding with which the Religious Society of Friends struggled, and on which it eventually came to a clear focus. In both cases the fundamental issues are the same: control and use of energy, economic productivity, convenience, aggrandizement, massive inequities, and the effect on the souls of all those who were and are enmeshed, in whatever capacity, in a system of unsustainable exploitation.

These similarities are not a coincidence. The end of slavery coincided with the full development of the machine-based factory system, expanding use of coal and the discovery of petroleum. The exploitive mindset and inequitable relationships of the old economy were continued in the new. This is why John Woolman's observations on economic behavior and social relations continue to be highly

15

pertinent to our time. Because the whole political economy was—and still is—driven by the unquestioned assumption of endless growth, no reflection on sustainable adaptation has ever gained a significant public hearing. The expanding frontier mentality and the vast "natural resources" of the North American continent allowed what historian William Appleman Williams called "the great evasion"—not taking fully into account the fundamental values, attitudes, and relationships required to achieve a sustainable pattern of settlement and economic activity within the regional ecosystems of the continent. That great evasion has continued unabated to the present time.

As the Religious Society of Friends rose to the issue of slavery and eventually became clear on the kind of change that was required, so it would seem we might now rise to the issue of ecological degradation in general and the situation of energy use and disruptive climate change in particular. Although it was certainly not easy for Friends to become collectively clear about slavery, it may be even more difficult to achieve a sense of clarity and undertake effective action with regard to ecological degradation.

When Friends voluntarily gave up slaveholding, the primary economic activity of farming could still be carried on with the human energy of hired labor, which, as Woolman so eloquently pointed out, must also be seen within a moral context. But with the subsequent shift of the economy to machine-based manufacturing, fueled by coal and oil, the cautionary moral dimension around energy use disappeared. And in fact, with the new technologies a new morality of energy use arose that said, in effect, "the more the better." We now understand this era of high energy use has been a terrible adaptational mistake. Despite the undeniable advances in convenience that high-energy living affords, the damaging impact of this adaptational stance on the biotic integrity of Earth has now, as in the days of slavery, brought the moral issue to a very fine point.

Addressing the issue of our energy use, and the way it exploits and damages Earth's communities of life, is a difficult matter. Virtually everyone in our society, in some way, is living off the pattern of energy production and use that is damaging Earth's biotic integrity and leading to increasing ecological disruption. Nothing less than a major re-adaptation of human settlement and economic activity is required to address this situation. Because the magnitude of our dilemma encompasses the whole adaptational stance of our culture, it reaches deeply into our spiritual life. It reaches right into the center of our understanding of ourselves within Creation.

16

In response to the spiritual dimension of our ecological dilemma, a movement of witness and action is growing in communities of faith worldwide. Many individual Friends are deeply immersed in this work, but the Religious Society of Friends, as a corporate expression of faith, has yet to move decisively into this spiritual task. Varieties of minutes have been formulated and approved. Special interest groups have arisen. Committees and working groups exist. Some yearly meetings are supporting the efforts of their members who are called to work for ecological reformation. As good as all these things are, it still leaves us with the question of why no yearly meeting or widely representative Friends organization has stepped into a leadership position on the integrity of Creation. In many instances individual Friends have been on the forefront of ecological reformation, but the Religious Society of Friends, as such, seems somewhat unfocused and muted on what is certainly one of the preeminent human dilemmas and critical dangers of our history. For a spiritual movement and community of faith that has been in the forefront of social innovation and human betterment for most of its history, this is a peculiar circumstance. One hopes that the old Spirit is just gathering strength and will, before long and at many collective points, move the Religious Society of Friends into clarity and action on behalf of Creation and a sustainable human/Earth relationship. Thus will all of our traditional concerns and areas of work find a helpful context and a renewed orientation.

In summary:

1) The science around global warming and disruptive climate change is clear.

2) The disruption by human activity of the biospheric conditions that have brought Earth's communities of life to their present interrelated existence is a direct and blasphemous challenge to the goodness of Creation. It is counterproductive to stable human settlement and sustainable economic activity. It is damaging to a sense of the Divine and to a viable, sustainable faith.

3) We have the technology and the skills to reconstruct human settlement and economic adaptation within ecologically sustainable norms.

4) At present we collectively lack the moral conviction, political will, and financial incentives needed to significantly advance the work of ecologically sustainable adaptation.

5) Communities of faith, by virtue of their claim on a relationship with the Divine, are under the obligation to provide leadership on the integrity of Creation issue and on the work of ecologically sustainable re-adaptation.

6) Despite the ecological work that many individual Friends, groups of Friends, and Friends meetings have been doing, the Religious Society of Friends in the United States is notably absent from the ecumenical associations and religious coalitions that are working on the human/Earth relationship and the integrity of Creation issue. Particularly with regard to addressing the ecological implications of public policy, this lack of Quaker participation in the wider religious dialogue would seem a lapse we should move to correct.

Can we transcend the special-interest view and the simplistic lifestyle response? Can we find a renewed sense of spiritual purpose in the task of reweaving all our concerns into a truly ecological worldview? Can we provide leadership in addressing public policy on behalf of the integrity of Creation? Can we engage the practical tasks of readapting our shelters, our settlements, and our social and economic systems to the biotic integrity of regional ecosystems and to the Earth as a whole?

Since this essay was published, FCNL has retrofitted its Washington headquarters to the highest standard of "green building" energy efficiency. Likewise, Friends Center in Philadelphia has completed extensive energy efficiency retrofitting and now stands as a prominent witness of the greening that can be done even with older buildings. In 2002, FCNL made energy and environmental policy one of its priorities, and its commitment to this work has been steadily strengthened. In 2004 American Friends Service Committee (AFSC) included a section on the environment in its Working Party report, *Putting Dignity and Rights at the Heart of the Global Economy: A Quaker Perspective*.[25]

In 2003, the Environmental Working Group of Philadelphia Yearly Meeting hosted a gathering of 29 Quaker economists, ecologists and policy professionals. The epistle[26] from that gathering follows:

Concerning Economic Policy and Friends Testimonies
A Letter from the Quaker Gathering on Economics and Ecology

Wallingford, Pennsylvania, June 2003

To Friends Everywhere,

We greet you as 29 individuals, belonging to 19 Monthly Meetings and 11 Yearly Meetings. Many among us are or have been actively involved with organizations such as the American Friends Service Committee, Canadian Friends Service Committee, Friends Association for Higher Education, Friends Committee on Unity with Nature, Quaker Eco-Witness, Friends Committee on National Legislation, Friends General Conference, and Friends World Committee for Consultation.

We have gathered at Pendle Hill to explore a concern we all share about economic policies as they relate to issues of peace, justice, equality, and restoring the earth's ecological integrity. We believe the human-earth relationship in all its aspects is inseparable from our relationship with the Divine. We are convinced that the current economic system should be of urgent concern to the Religious Society of Friends. It is intensifying economic and social inequities throughout the world, causing structural and physical violence, driving many species to extinction, and leading our own species toward ecological self-destruction.

Through our worshipful deliberations, we have come to unity in urging all Friends, especially those in the United States and Canada, to make individual and corporate commitments to learning more about certain fundamental aspects of current economic policies and institutions as they relate to Friends' historic testimonies. Specifically, we encourage Friends to ask themselves the following:

In light of Friends' Testimonies, what is God calling us to do about the continuing and increasing marginalization of so much of the world's population, the extinction of species, and other environmental degradation? How do we integrate our human community within the natural world so as to provide for the physical and spiritual needs of future generations?

What changes in the institutions of economy and governance are needed to promote effective stewardship of the natural environment and caring for people and communities?

What is it in nature and human knowledge that we have the right to own?

How best can we promote the values expressed in the Universal Declaration of Human Rights and the Earth Charter? How can we promote understanding and awareness of the consequences of increasing global interconnectedness and the urgency of addressing the dangers and opportunities that these present?

As we earn, spend, and invest money, as individuals and as meeting communities, how can we live in the "virtue of that life and power" that leads us to treat all humans and the Earth as a manifestation of the Divine? Are we aware of the true cost of our consumption? Do we take into account our concerns for social justice as we earn, spend, and invest money?

What information, tools, and skills do we need to equip ourselves to work effectively for public policies that restore Earth's resilience, increase social equity, and strengthen community?

How can we engage with others in ways that help us discern God's will for us, at this critical stage in Earth's history, as we labor with these concerns?

Quaker Eco-Witness, a project of Friends Committee on Unity with Nature, and the Environmental Working Group of Philadelphia Yearly Meeting have collaborated in bringing us to Pendle Hill. They will also collaborate with us in preparing a collection of short articles, questions to help clarify Friends' understanding, and queries to encourage Friends' individual and corporate discernment about the concerns we raise. We have agreed to pursue a number of tasks designed to create and draw together existing material on economics and ecology as resources for our meetings and wider communities. We hope you will make use of these materials when they become available in the late fall or early winter.

In the Light,
Elaine C. Emmi, Recording Clerk

One outcome of this gathering was *Seeds of Violence, Seeds of Hope*, a resource of core readings, workshop activities, and in-depth perspectives on economic issues, which was published in three volumes between 2005 and 2007. Establishing the Quaker Institute for the Future

(QIF)[27] was another outcome of this gathering. In 2009 QIF published a flagship book, *Right Relationship: Building a Whole Earth Economy.*[28] The book asks and answers five basic questions: What is the economy for? How does the economy work? How big should the economy be? What's fair? How should the economy be governed? It concludes with a chapter on grassroots strategy for change, "Four Steps to a Whole Earth Economy."

The next year the Growth Dilemma Project developed the "Core Principles for a Quaker Witness on Ecology and the Economy,"[29] which were accepted by Philadelphia Yearly Meeting in Session, March, 2010.

Core Principles for a Quaker Witness on Ecology and the Economy
The Growth Dilemma Project of Philadelphia Yearly Meeting, March 2010

As Quakers, we recognize our interconnectedness with the earth. Yet, we see that humans are exceeding the earth's carrying capacity: ecosystems are collapsing; species are disappearing at an accelerating rate.

We value equality. Yet we see economic inequality increasing dramatically, both nationally and internationally, poverty begetting deeper poverty, and the environs of the poor being degraded while consumption by the affluent keeps rising.

We value integrity. Yet the growth of Gross Domestic Product (GDP), which drives our policies, is a false measure of prosperity because it includes spending on waste and destruction we ourselves create. To be truthful, our measures must reflect all social and environmental costs, including costs to future generations of our uses and abuses of earth's resources.

We value simplicity, living within one's means, and leaving places better than we find them, as important for mental and spiritual health. Yet, our "growth economy" requires ever-increasing spending, consumer debt, and intrusion on the natural world to sustain itself.

We value community and look toward the Kingdom of God on Earth. Yet, the number of people without secure employment, without health insurance, and confined to prisons is increasing, while the community of life, created by God and to which we belong, is steadily diminished.

We value peace. Yet the worldwide strife and devastation caused by our dependence on fossil fuels is alarming. The seeds of deadly conflict have nourishment in our energy-intensive life-styles.

Something is deeply awry. What, after all, is the economy for?

Surely it should not be just to give the wealthiest among us more wealth and more power.

Surely it should not be just to maximize profits by eliminating the jobs that people need.

Surely it should not be to convince us we need things we are better off without.

Surely it should not be to strip the earth of its resources, pollute it with our wastes, and make life untenable for the most vulnerable.

We believe that by any religious, moral, or ethical standard, our economy should serve all our people, the children who come after us, and the commonwealth of life on which our existence depends. Let us seek and speak the truth about the failures of our current system more openly and boldly. Let us come together to learn what is needed, and to make use of what we learn, to bring our economy into right relationship with the ideals of our history, the welfare of our posterity, and the well-being of our only earth.

The Friends World Committee on Consultation carried out an extensive two-year consultation with Friends worldwide in preparation for the April 2012 6th World Conference of Friends at Kabarak University in Kenya. The result was "The Kabarak Call for Peace and Ecojustice."[30]

The Kabarak Call for Peace and Ecojustice

The Kabarak Call for Peace and Ecojustice was approved on 24 April 2012 at the Sixth World Conference Friends, held at Kabarak University near Nakuru, Kenya. It is being circulated with the Conference Epistle.

In past times God's Creation restored itself. Now humanity dominates, our growing population consuming more resources than nature can replace. We must change, we must become careful stewards of all life. Earthcare unites traditional Quaker testimonies: peace, equality, simplicity, love, integrity, and justice. Jesus said,

"As you have done unto the least… you have done unto me". We are called to work for the peaceable Kingdom of God on the whole earth, in right sharing with all peoples. However few our numbers, we are called to be the salt that flavours and preserves, to be a light in the darkness of greed and destruction.

We have heard of the disappearing snows of Kilimanjaro and glaciers of Bolivia, from which come life-giving waters. We have heard appeals from peoples of the Arctic, Asia and Pacific. We have heard of forests cut down, seasons disrupted, wildlife dying, of land hunger in Africa, of new diseases, droughts, floods, fires, famine and desperate migrations—this climatic chaos is now worsening. There are wars and rumors of war, job loss, inequality and violence. We fear our neighbors. We waste our children's heritage.

All of these are driven by our dominant economic systems—by greed not need, by worship of the market, by Mammon and Caesar.

Is this how Jesus showed us to live?

We are called to see what love can do: to love our neighbor as ourselves, to aid the widow and orphan, to comfort the afflicted, to appeal to consciences and bind the wounds.

We are called to teach our children right relationship, to live in harmony with each other and all living beings in the earth, waters and sky of our Creator, who asks, "Where were you when I laid the foundations of the world?" (Job 38:4)

We are called to do justice to all and walk humbly with our God, to cooperate lovingly with all who share our hopes for the future of the earth.

We are called to be patterns and examples in a 21st century campaign for peace and ecojustice, as difficult and decisive as the 19th century drive to abolish slavery.

We dedicate ourselves to let the living waters flow through us—where we live, regionally, and in wider world fellowship. We dedicate ourselves to building the peace that passeth all understanding, to the repair of the world, opening our lives to the Light to guide us in each small step.

Praise God. Bwana asifiwe. Apu Dios Awqui. Gracias Jesús. Jubilé. Salaam aleikum. Migwetch.

CHAPTER TWO

Elements of an Economic System

Ed Dreby and Margaret Mansfield

Forty-five years ago Kenneth Boulding identified the need to adapt our society and economy to a smaller and more crowded Earth (*pp 8-12*). Since then we have seen the physical expansion of human enterprise with minimal consideration of ecological balance. With no "empty place" left to settle, we confront the limitations of the global habitat.

Clearly the human population cannot continue to grow forever. Nor can the amount of land humans use, or the number of houses, cars, roads, and factories we build. Yet our public policies continue to promote, and require, economic growth as a solution to our problems. Only a few economists have begun to consider what needs to be done to fit the now global economy into the biosphere.

There are two clear trends occurring in today's regional economies and the global economy:

- The expansion of human economic activities is damaging regional and global ecosystems, and

- The wealthiest are becoming wealthier and the number of impoverished people is increasing.

While economic expansion has a direct and obvious effect on ecosystems and resources, so do extremes of wealth and poverty. These factors contribute to violent conflicts, which in turn devastate ecosystems. If one considers cause and effect, then concern for peace, social justice, and protecting the biosphere must be intertwined.

This chapter describes some of the basic concepts of modern economics that are useful for considering what lies beneath these problematic trends.

Factors of production: Economists traditionally identify three basic factors of production: the resources from land, labor contributed by households, and capital.

Capital: A simple definition of capital is wealth used to increase the ability to produce. Orthodox economists distinguish between:

- ***real capital***, or "physical capital," encompasses the tools, machines, buildings, trucks, roads and bridges used to produce and distribute more and better goods and services; and

- ***financial capital***, the savings in the form of cash, stocks, bonds, and other financial securities that are used to pay for manufactured capital.

Entrepreneurs use financial capital to produce real capital, and then to pay for the resources and labor needed to make a marketable product, all for the purpose of making a profit because the price of the product is more than the price of its costs

Investment: For the economy as a whole, an investment refers to spending for new real capital: a new tool, machine, building, truck, road, or bridge. If the investment is successful, there will be an increase in the goods or services provided for people who want them, and a profit for the business. For an individual, an investment is taking the risk of using savings to own or loan in the business sector.

Market: A market is the system that brings buyers and sellers together to freely exchange goods and services. If there are many buyers and sellers, prices tend to be fair and the outcome efficient. If there are only a few sellers or buyers, markets can result in unfairly high or low prices and inefficient allocation of resources and distribution of goods.

In a modern industrial economy, people don't make things for themselves, but instead use income from their wages, salaries, and savings to buy products and services in the marketplace. In addition to markets for goods and services, there are markets for land, labor, and a great many different kinds of capital. If the society is to prosper, it is important for markets to function fairly and efficiently.

Money and its circulation: Money circulates in a market economy between businesses and households, as do the goods and services for which money is exchanged. Much of contemporary economics focuses on analyzing the flows of goods, services, and money in markets, which are represented in their most simple form by a Simple Circular Flow Diagram (*Figure 1*).

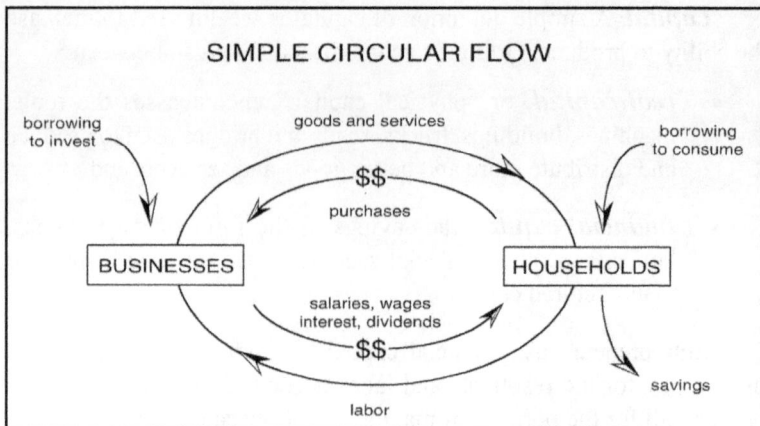

Figure 1. Simple Circular Flow (Kim Carlyle, *Seeds of Violence, Seeds of Hope,* Vol. 1)

Prosperity is created when goods, services, and money are cycled between businesses and households. If more money enters the markets relative to the volume and rate of goods and services being exchanged, then prices will tend to rise and the value of the money will become less. This is what is meant by *inflation.* In times of inflation, money tends to lose its usefulness as a store of value.

If the money supply is reduced so there is less money relative to goods and services, then theoretically prices will go down (deflation). More commonly, reductions in the money supply have tended to reduce or depress the level of economic activity. This is one cause of a *recession.*

Savings: When people decide to save part of their income instead of spending it, their savings are temporarily withdrawn from the circular flow. Savings may be returned to the flow in two basic ways: they may be invested in the business sector to finance new development, or they may be borrowed by another household for consumption. In either case, people expect to receive a return on their savings in the form of interest, dividends, or rent.

Interest: Interest is money a borrower pays a lender in exchange for being able to use borrowed financial capital over a period of time. When people put savings in a bank to earn interest, they are actually lending the money to the bank, which is in business to lend other people's money. In a market economy, dividends, rents and other financial returns serve functions similar to interest payments.

Organization of Orthodox Economics

There are two branches of orthodox economics and two analytic orientations.

Microeconomics focuses on specific markets and how they are affected by the choices made by consumers, producers, and governments. (*See Microeconomics: Markets and Choice*)

Macroeconomics focuses on understanding what influences the overall level of economic activity on regional, national, and global scales. (*See Macroeconomics: Modern Industrial Economies*)

Positive analysis views economics as a value-free science, and attempts to provide objective descriptions, often by using mathematical models, to describe how economies actually function and to predict outcomes that match real world experience.

Normative analysis views economics as a social science, and uses theory and empirical findings, combined with value-based perceptions and insights, to promote a given perspective on economic policy.

Ecological Economics

Another approach to economics is Ecological Economics, an emerging field in which Kenneth Boulding's ideas have been formative. Ecological economists use models that place the economy in the larger context of the social world and Earth's ecosystems in which it functions. They say human economies must be re-designed as closed systems in which all populations have sustainable niches and all matter is recycled.

Ecological economists view capital much more broadly, as a physical stock that can provide the economy with a flow of useful resources. Ecological economists refer to real capital as "*manufactured capital*," and they highlight other kinds of capital that are also needed to produce goods and services. Large corporations have become concerned about the *human capital* available to them, the knowledge and skills of a region's workforce acquired through education and training. They use multilateral enforcement of patents to protect their *intellectual capital*, their new knowledge. For ecological economists, two other kinds of capital are of essential importance, natural capital and social capital. *Natural capital* includes all the physical resources from Earth's ecosystems. *Social capital* includes the trust, expectations and interactive skills developed in families, communities, organizations, and business operations.

Each of these forms of capital provides important flows of useful material and energy. Ecological economists ask how market economies can be structured to assure that investments are made to maintain and enhance not only the stocks of manufactured and financial capital, but also the stocks of natural and social capital. Figure 2 illustrates a more accurate and complex model.

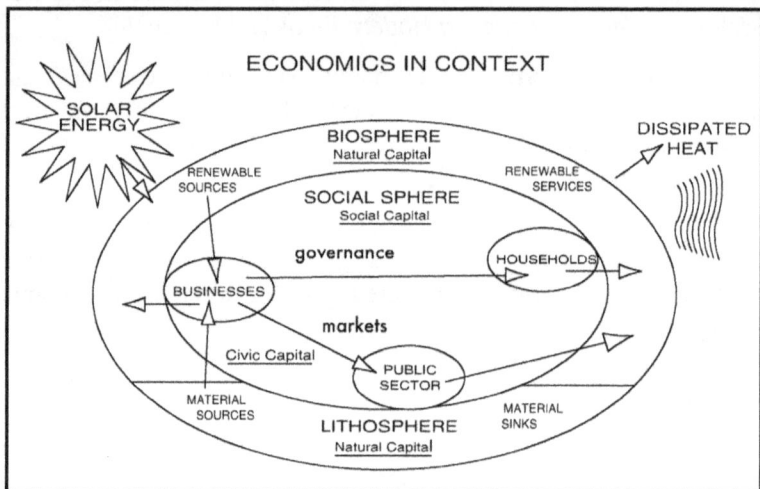

Figure 2. Economics in Context (Kim Carlyle, *Seeds of Violence, Seeds of Hope,* Vol. 1)

Many political leaders, and the public at large, are very concerned about dealing with social and environmental problems. Yet few people think about the economy in the causes of social and environmental problems, about the need to invest in the economy's natural and social capital.

If an economic system is to prosper, its stocks of manufactured capital must be maintained or replaced. A company that begins selling its machinery without replacing it, or begins to "liquidate" its capital stock, will produce fewer goods and services. Ecological economists observe that this is also true of natural and social capital. A society and its economy that doesn't maintain its natural and social capital as well as its manufactured capital, will sooner or later go out of business.

Microeconomics: Markets and Choices
David Ross and Ed Dreby

To understand economics in its fullest sense means recognizing that we must make choices about spending time and money, collaborating with one another, caring for our surroundings, and participating in our communities. Sharing food at a potluck, composting in the garden, turning on a light to read a good book, or attending a municipal hearing, we get something we want, and give up something to get it. Each has economic benefits and costs.

We easily ignore this reality because we tend to associate economics only with money and markets. And indeed, orthodox economics does focus on money and markets, which mediates many of the choices that dominate daily life in industrial economies.

Because industrial economies are complex, interdependent, and subject to unexpected changes, macroeconomics has not had notable success as a predictive science. Microeconomics, on the other hand, has produced accepted economic principles about how markets function. Our purpose here is to describe the most basic concepts of microeconomics.

What is a Market?

A "market" refers to the process by which buyers and sellers agree on prices for the goods and services they exchange. In the pre-industrial world, markets were a small part of the economy. Most decisions to produce or consume were made in households or villages, or by the decree of someone in authority. Markets became the basis for organizing economic life as innovations in communication and transportation allowed larger groups of people to interact with one another. This greatly enhanced the benefits from specializing in producing particular goods and services. As market-based economics developed, so did the need to understand them. For this reason, markets have become a major focus of economics as a field of study.

All choices have consequences. According to economic theory, the opportunities we forego as a result of choices we make are among the economic costs we incur—opportunity costs such as the road not taken, the shirt we didn't buy, the hungry people we failed to feed—because time and resources are limited.

Formal economic theory is constructed as if each of us makes rational choices. According to the theory, we don't do things for which the additional costs exceed the additional benefits. Benefits and costs are related to scarcity. If something becomes less scarce, its benefit decreases and its opportunity cost increases. A familiar version of this relationship is the "law of diminishing returns." You may be eager for one bowl of ice cream, but are you as eager for a third, fourth, or fifth?

Benefits and costs are also related to the perception of risk. If you value the safety of your children, why do you let them ride in the car with you? Because you don't think the risk of an accident is very high, especially if you are driving. No society has ever chosen to eliminate all air pollution, because the cost is perceived as too high in relation to the perceived benefit of the economic activity producing the pollution. Economics is about tradeoffs between costs and benefits.

Buying and selling in markets can lower the costs of many things we desire. Life would be pretty grim if each family needed a goat for its milk and had to transform rock and fiber into shelter, clothes and paper. Sharing our possessions and dividing our tasks among family and friends are ways to solve this problem on a small scale. Markets divide tasks and share goods and services on a much larger and more impersonal scale.

Adam Smith, who is viewed as the father of economics, used an example of a pin factory he visited. The business of making a pin was "divided into about eighteen distinct operations ... all performed by distinct hands. ... But if they had all wrought separately and independently, ... they certainly could not each of them make twenty, perhaps not one pin a day."[31]

Markets enable society to reduce costs and increase benefits by promoting the division of labor and specialization. By devoting our energies to tasks that we can do relatively faster or better than someone else, and then exchanging the fruits of our labor (indirectly as wage employees, or directly by selling what we produce), we reduce the costs of daily life and enjoy material well-being beyond our ancestor's wildest dreams.

Microeconomic analysis describes the complexity of economic relations as the interplay of many different markets. Households operate in markets for employment, goods and services, and earnings on their savings. Businesses operate in markets for land, labor, real capital, and financial capital. Governments are also major participants in markets, and financial institutions have recently developed many new markets for new products.

Supply and Demand

Economists refer to allocation, scale, and distribution to describe the decisions made by markets: ***allocation*** refers to what gets produced and what is used to produce it, ***scale*** to how much gets produced, and ***distribution*** to who gets it.

If buyers want more than suppliers are producing, the price will rise and producers will have an incentive to increase production. If costs of production and, therefore, prices rise, buyers will make different choices and demand will fall. This is referred to as ***elasticity of supply and demand***. For sellers, if the supply of an essential factor of production is limited, or its cost is too high, expanding production may not be profitable or possible, and the supply of the product will be relatively ***inelastic***. For buyers, if the product is essential to survival, they may be willing, or forced, to pay higher prices, and the demand will be relatively ***inelastic***.

In markets, large groups of individuals usually respond collectively to prices and income incentives as if people pursue their self-interest. Following self-interest usually drives markets in the direction of forcing the quantity supplied of any good to just equal the quantity demanded. An ideal fully functioning market involves unique goods and services, and many well-informed buyers and sellers. From the laws of supply and demand, fully functioning markets would result in an economy where individuals choose among the greatest range of goods and services at the lowest feasible price.

What Markets Provide and Promote

Voluntary exchange: The theoretical essence of a market is that both the buyer and the seller gain. The buyer must expect to be better off with the product, and the seller must expect to be better off with the money received. Otherwise, there would be no exchange. This is the case whether the participants are individuals, households, or nations. When China sends gambling machines to the U.S. in return for dollars, China must "believe" it can buy other goods with those dollars that will serve its needs better than keeping the gambling machines for its own use.

31

In the absence of close relationships and communal unity, market exchange is the most effective means humans have devised for sharing goods and services among large numbers of people. A high price for something communicates that there are people in the society who would welcome more of it. A high price also means that buying the product will decrease one's ability to buy other things. In an ideal world, sharing would be based on spiritual unity, mutual understanding, and love. But history is full of examples where communal outcomes are driven instead by shaming, stereotyping, or the will of the powerful.

Efficiency in the use of resources: The ideal market is efficient in the sense that resources are used to provide consumers with the quality and quantity of goods based on their willingness to pay. At the price at which quantity supplied equals the quantity demanded, the cost of providing one more unit is just equal to the benefit. That is, it is clear to everyone in an ideal market those additional costs just equal additional benefits. Everyone is pleased with the outcome. Unfortunately, no such certainty exists for real choices made within real families, corporations, communities, or nations.

Productivity and innovation: To stay in business, producers must provide what the markets demand, and at the lowest possible cost. Innovations bring increased productivity and lower costs. Innovations attract new buyers. Entrepreneurs look for new opportunities to make a profit, and in doing so, invest in new physical capital. But profitable markets are also eroded by innovations. Hence, innovation tends to turn markets toward the "survival of the fittest."

Market Failure

There are a host of circumstances under which markets fail in their coordinating task: there is too little or too much produced, the capabilities of human beings are wasted, and gifts of the natural world are abused or wasted. Theoretically, markets that function well would use everyone's labor to its best advantage. But, we know this doesn't happen in practice. We see much harm in the blighted, ad-polluted world around us. No economy has ever relied exclusively on market exchange. We must use other institutions to correct for market failures without undermining the ability of markets to serve our interests.

Positive Economic Analysis

From the perspective of positive economic analysis, the breadth and magnitude of social injustice and environmental degradation is the result of multiple market failures and the lack of political will or capacity to correct them. Markets fail in three basic ways: 1) by not restraining negative externalities, 2) by not providing public goods, and 3) by not preventing excessive market concentration.

Negative externalities are the costs that are external to a market transaction. That is, they are costs to a third party, rather than to the seller or buyer, that neither the buyer nor seller pays. For example, there would be significant costs to a home owner if a gas station opened next to it: more traffic and air pollution, noise pollution, chemical poisoning, and a probable loss in resale value of the home.

Negative externalities occur when production results in pollution. The pollution may be hazardous to workers, the neighborhood, those living downwind or downstream, the public at large, or the environment as a whole, and to future generations. Because businesses do not bear the cost of externalities in their accounting systems, they charge too little for their products, sell too much of them, and make profits at others' expense. Markets tend to promote negative externalities, because an obvious way to cut costs is to shift them to others. Government intervention is almost always needed to make producers "internalize" the costs of pollution.

Public goods benefit many people without distinguishing between those who pay and those who don't. In most market transactions, the seller transfers to the buyer the exclusive right to use the good or service. For example, anyone in the neighborhood can enjoy the fireworks on the Fourth of July, and one person's enjoyment does not diminish another's, but probably increases it instead. Although a fireworks display has a real cost, if everyone can see it without paying for it, the market has no way to cover the cost.

Market concentration refers to markets in which a few parties buy or sell most of the product. This enables one or a few of the parties to set prices much higher than costs. Big companies often have economies of scale so that more is produced for consumers at a lower cost. But a big company can also take unfair advantage in buying raw materials, hiring employees, and marketing goods products, thereby making higher profits at the expense of suppliers, employees, and consumers. And the goal of most companies is to monopolize their markets.

Failures arising from market concentration provide the logic for antitrust legislation, government regulation, and social or community ownership. Too much market concentration, and the accumulation of wealth it fosters, can also be used to influence government policies. In a vicious cycle, corporations may use excess profits to lobby for public policies that further increase their power in the markets.

Multiple market failures often occur, especially in the area of ecosystem protection. Within the analytic framework of economics, most ecosystem services are public goods, and most environmental harms are caused by negative externalities. Market concentration creates political influence that can block efforts to correct for negative externalities and provide for public goods. Manufacturers lobby against pollution prevention and developers against wetlands preservation. Market failures result in harm to the many and benefits to the few.

Normative and Ecological Perspectives

From a normative perspective based on the values implicit in Quaker testimonies (simplicity, peace, integrity, community, equality), additional failures of the market system are of critical importance to societies and the human-Earth relationship.

Markets promote materialism: The view that markets benefit the society as a whole depends on the assumption that people always act in their own best interest. It also assumes that no one can force or manipulate someone else into making a bad choice. Do our relationships based on market exchange replace those based on mutual caring? Does manipulative advertising influence our buying habits? These are examples that Economist David George calls "preference pollution," meaning that our day-to-day desires and actions have been manipulated in ways that are inconsistent with our self-interest, our spiritual values or what we would choose from a place of reflection. [32]

Change can hurt: Innovation, ingenuity, and the human capacity to learn are constantly expanding our understanding of what is possible. New enterprises are created while others shut down in a process Joseph Schumpeter named, "creative destruction." Absent altruism or government intervention, many are hurt by innovations and the social change that results. Not only can change destroy communities and jobs, it can destroy the ecosystem. The balance between innovation and stability is hard to find.

Markets tend to create economic inequities: The income distribution that emerges through market exchange is usually unequal because markets tend toward a "winner-take-all" outcome. The impersonal nature of markets masks the sources of inequities and injustice in the distribution of wealth. Extremes of wealth and poverty damage the well-being of rich and poor alike. Disadvantaged people are unable to pursue their own best interests in market exchanges, so they are marginalized even further.

Material sprawl: Efficient markets determine how much consumers will purchase, but they do nothing to restrain consumption. The profit motive in markets leads businesses to make as much as possible of whatever they can sell, and to induce consumers to buy as much as they can with their income and available credit. The result can be a society with huge material excesses and high levels of poverty.

Speculation: Markets provide opportunities to buy something solely in anticipation that its price will rise and they will be able to sell and reap an "unearned" profit. This is a phenomenon akin to gambling with all its potentially addictive consequences. Recent crises in the housing and financial markets have presented a challenging research topic for academic economists.

Markets and Public Policy

Policy interventions to correct for market failures have typically been of three kinds: 1) regulations, 2) preferential taxes, and 3) preferential subsidies. Government can prohibit certain activities, or only permit them to a limited degree or under limited conditions. Government can have an impact by taxing undesirable goods more than desirable, and by paying individuals or companies to do some things and not other things.

In the past few years, the regulatory toolkit has expanded to include ***tradable permits*** that use a market to control negative externalities or provide public goods. Reducing the number of permits over time reduces emissions while letting industries and the market determine how best to do it. Tradable permits reduced sulfur emissions more quickly at lower cost than most analysts expected. Adapting this approach to proposals for reducing carbon emissions is proving to be more difficult.

Unintended Consequences: Policy interventions often lead to unexpected results. Some are beneficial and others are detrimental. The logic of supply and demand in the marketplace is powerful. Like a flood or lava flow, it overwhelms or bypasses all obstacles, often in ways that would have been difficult to predict in advance. Rent control tended to reduce the quality and availability of rental housing, which increased the homelessness it was designed to reduce. Mandating higher fuel efficiency for automobiles has turned exempted "commercial" trucks into gas-guzzling SUVs. Mandatory recycling has spawned a host of new products. The Internet, originally created to maintain emergency communications, has become an engine for the entire growth economy.

Cost-benefit Analysis

Cost-benefit analysis is a process of weighing costs against benefits as potential outcomes of a particular action or policy. It can help individuals and policymakers in business and government reach prudent decisions. It is one of the most useful tools of microeconomic analysis for assessment of proposed economic regulations and developmental projects.

The National Environmental Policy Act of 1969 requires the filing of environmental impact assessments (EIAs) for all Federal projects and the Office of Management and Budget requires all Federal agencies to consider the economic impact of their actions and to choose the policy alternative that minimizes the costs to society.

In theory, environmental or economic impact statements bring together all of the relevant data to determine the impact of proposed projects or regulations to allow government officials to make appropriate decisions. Cost-benefit analysis makes assumptions about the efficiency of markets, the various non-market (externalized) costs, and the risks of accident, disease or death.

In practice, however, conclusions from cost-benefit analysis are determined by the assumptions. Anything entered into analysis must be measured in quantitative terms, but the claim sometimes made that cost-benefit analysis is objective is not accurate. Both industry and government forecasts tend to overestimate the costs of compliance with regulations, while advocates for regulatory policies tend to overestimate the quantifiable benefits. Preparers of EIAs might meet the letter of the law, but bury information about serious environmental effects in long, detailed reports so that busy government decision-makers will read only executive summaries. For many social and environmental problems, the conclusions from all but the most biased calculations are not even close calls. The harm to societal well-being from the most unregulated market failures vastly exceeds the costs of controlling them.

Conclusion

When markets function well, they do a good job of exchanging goods and services for a large, diverse population. However, market failures interfere with the efficiency of market exchange, with damaging consequences for society and the environment. Community action and government policies are the only ways to correct most market failures. Yet nothing ensures that political processes will yield outcomes that protect people and the planet.

Microeconomics focuses only on markets. If economic activities create inequitable distribution and damage ecosystems, it is because public policy has not corrected the market failures caused by excessive negative externalities and market concentration. It is macroeconomics that considers public policy, which we will discuss next.

Meeting our spiritually-based stewardship obligations requires good choices at both the individual and policy levels. Many tools exist to reshape the marketplace to be more ecologically sound and socially just. How can we encourage the use of the economists' tools in these ways?

Macroeconomics:
Industrial Economies as Systems
Ed Dreby and Margaret Mansfield

Throughout the history of market-based industrial economies there have been periods of stability, boom, and bust. Explanations about why this happens involve money, banking, weather, new inventions, new infrastructure, various business practices, and speculation. The most severe of these busts was the Great Depression of the 1930s.

Macroeconomic analysis originated in the theories developed by British Economist John Maynard Keynes to understand what caused it, why it lasted so long, and how to avoid a similar collapse in the future. Macroeconomic analysis is centered on two basic insights about the way industrial economies function. The first is that the relationship between savings and investment is a key determinant of the overall level of economic activity. The second is that a market system has many positive feedback mechanisms that accentuate tendencies to expand or contract, and lacks internal negative feedback mechanisms to provide stability.

Why Do Modern Economies Tend to Expand?

Modern industrial economies tend to expand because of the relationship between savings and investment. When people decide to save part of their income instead of spending it for goods and services, the income saved is temporarily withheld from markets. To the degree that savings are withdrawn from the circular flow, the money in circulation is reduced and the demand for goods and services is apt to decline.

Savings can be returned to the circular flow in one of two ways. They may be deposited in a bank to earn interest, in which case they are apt to be loaned by the bank, and then be returned to the circular flow by the borrower's spending. Or they may be used in financial markets to help support new investment.

To the degree that savings are restored to the circular flow, whether for investment or consumption, the level of demand will be sustained. Furthermore, borrowers will have to increase their future economic activity to repay the loan plus interest, and this is apt to make the economy grow.

But if savings are not being borrowed and used for consumption and investment, overall spending will be reduced. If there is not enough spending to buy the goods and services that businesses produce or plan to produce, businesses are apt to reduce employment. This in turn is apt to further reduce household spending, and lead to a recession.

Thus, to prevent recessions, governments want businesses to borrow for investment, and businesses want consumers to borrow for consumption.

Positive and Negative Feedbacks

The second insight of macroeconomic analysis is that modern industrial economies contain many positive feedback mechanisms and lack negative feedback mechanisms. Positive feedback is when a mechanism in the system responds to a change by causing more change of the same sort. Negative feedback is when a mechanism responds to change by countering, or compensating for the effect of the change, which stabilizes the system.

In economics, positive feedback does not necessarily lead to a positive outcome, especially in the long run. More of a good thing, economic expansion for example, may be welcomed for a time, but sooner or later the system will be destabilized, and economic contraction will lead to more contraction.

There are many systemic elements of industrial economies that have the potential to create positive feedback that harms society, such as:

- a concentration of wealth tends to beget more concentration of wealth;

- if the economy is expanding, more savings and borrowing increases the money supply which feeds more expansion;

- if the economy is contracting, less saving and borrowing decreases the money supply which feeds more contraction;

- when speculative financial markets are booming, people's exuberance feeds the boom; and

- when the boom falters, people's pessimism feeds the faltering and may lead to a collapse.

There is an underlying irony in these positive feedbacks. An increase in production, employment, consumption and investment will sooner or later exceed the desire or ability of society to use all that businesses produce, and expansion yields to contraction. Furthermore, as fewer people own more of the wealth, the market failure of insufficient demand takes hold. These are the reasons for the system's fundamental instability.

When spending declines, business inventories increase, and production, employment and investment are reduced. A "vicious cycle" of economic decline may take hold, in which businesses are simply unwilling to borrow enough and banks unwilling to lend enough to reverse the decline. In 2012, the U.S. and the global economies are now contending with this circumstance.

Economists, politicians, and pundits disagree about what is most influential in creating instability, and how the instability should be managed, but because of positive feedbacks, it is now widely understood that continual expansion is needed to maintain prosperity.

Macroeconomic Analysis and Public Policy

Three elements interact to determine the overall level of economic activity:

1) private sector spending including consumer spending, business investment, and the financial markets;

2) public-sector government taxation, spending, and debt for consumption and investment; and

3) money supply and interest rates.

Macroeconomic analysis deals primarily with public policy because the role of government in shaping the economy is understood to be central.

Government taxation affects household spending and savings, business investment and production, and profits from financial speculation. Government spending for public consumption and investment affects overall demand, employment, public debt, interest rates and the money supply. Government monetary policy affects all of the above by influencing the level of spending, investment, and debt through increasing or decreasing the money supply and interest rates.

Orthodox economists agree on the goal of maintaining economic prosperity, and there is an assumption that sustaining economic prosperity means sustaining economic expansion. However, there is no agreement among economists about how the actions of government affect the economy, and what the government's role in the economy should be.

Four Approaches to Government Economic Policies

There are four main approaches to economic policy. Two are orthodox approaches in the mainstream of economic thought; and two are alternative approaches. Within what has been termed the "Washington consensus," the Neo-Keynesian approach derived from the Keynes school of thought advocates a strong government role in managing the economy using fiscal and monetary policy. In contrast, also among the mainstream economists, the Neo-Liberal approach advocates a minimal government role in managing the economy.

The Social Justice/Social Democratic and Ecological Economics are alternative approaches that seem essential to consider in the context of concerns about Friends' testimonies and the human-Earth relationship. Both reject the Washington consensus, and call for strong government intervention based on different assumptions and values.

Neo-Keynesian Approach. This activist approach attributes the sustained period of economic prosperity from the end of World War II to the Vietnam War to the successful implementation of Keynesian theories, which proposed that government intentionally use fiscal and monetary policy to act to balance the problems induced by positive feedback of unregulated markets. Government spending for consumption and investment, and the redistribution of income and wealth through taxation should be designed to maintain consumer demand, growth of income, and full employment. Keynesian policies are based on the following general ideas:

- If spending in the employment and private sectors is too low, the government should decrease taxes to increase private spending, and increase government debt so as to increase government spending;

41

- If there is already full employment and private sector spending is high enough to cause inflation, government should reduce its spending and raise taxes to moderate overall spending, which also reduces government debt;

- Taxation should be used to redistribute wealth to prevent the failure of insufficient demand; and

- Monetary policy should give priority to promoting high employment through lower interest rates.

Neo-Liberal Approach. The Neo-Liberal approach is to minimize the role of government in the economy. This developed from the work of Milton Friedman and his colleagues at the University of Chicago in the 1960s. The Neo-Liberalists reject the view that post-World War II prosperity was due to government policy and attribute the Federal Reserve's success in controlling the inflation of the 1970s and the economic recovery of the 1980s to the growing influence of Neo-Liberal policies.

This approach sees government intervention as too cumbersome to be timely, and holds that because cutting taxes is always easier than raising them, Keynesian policies simply increase government debt. Neo-Liberalists believe that government intervention inexorably leads to larger, less efficient, and more intrusive government, that government should:

- limit its role in managing the economy to providing for stable money supply and appropriate short-term interest rates, and

- set tax and spending policies on the basis of its legitimate and limited needs, and allow markets to determine the level of employment and distribution of wealth as long as the money supply is stable.

Social Justice/Social Democratic Approach. A diverse group of economists identify themselves as "heterodox" because they challenge assumptions of the "orthodox" Keynesians and neo-liberals. Many heterodox economists respond to what they perceive as systemic economic injustices that are tacitly condoned by orthodox theory. Some, though not all, are influenced by the contributions of Karl Marx and Max Weber on the economics of social class. This approach is more common among economists in Europe than in the U.S., and also among economic sociologists and geographers. It is broadly concerned with:

42

- a dynamic of exploitation in markets of weaker interests by the profit-seeking of more powerful interests;

- the accumulation of wealth, and its political influence to minimize regulations and taxes, and make wages, benefits and expenditures for social programs as low as possible;

- the need for public policy to provide rational oversight for private investment to assure that the general welfare takes precedent over profit-seeking;

- the need for stakeholder participation in the governance of corporations; and

- the need for strong public policies to protect against the effects of market-driven instabilities.

Ecological Economics Approach. Ecological economists hold that conventional economics is flawed because its models treat the environment as an externality, whereas in reality the human economies are wholly owned subsidiaries of the Earth's ecosphere. Specifically, orthodox economics doesn't account for the full costs of goods and services, and treats depletion of natural capital as income rather than as expense. Using GNP as the measure of prosperity, conventional economics does not measure real human well-being.

Ecological economists see a need, at regional, national and global levels, for:

- major investments in restoring and increasing the productivity of natural capital;

- including the real cost of using non-renewable resources, including the cost of the pollution generated in procuring the resources; and

- market mechanisms that provide feedbacks to establish and maintain ecologically sustainable limits to energy and material throughput.

The logical conclusions of the ecologically oriented analysis are that:

- The physical expansion of human economies in terms of material wealth will sooner or later end;

- Renewable throughput must not exceed Earth's sustainable yield and restorative capacities;
- The use of non-renewable raw materials, such as, metals, mineral, and fossil fuels, must be minimized;
- The energy throughput of human economies must come primarily from renewable sources;
- The concepts of capital, efficiency, and productivity, must be redefined to place economic activities in a context of ecological process; and
- Economic and social incentives must reward choices that restore, protect, and enhance Earth's biological productivity.

To date, this view has received greater support from ecologists, and from community development and social justice professionals than from economists.

Envisioning an economy that functions in right relationship with the commonwealth of life

It is perfectly possible, though not a simple matter, to devise an economy in which savings can be used for investment without driving economic expansion. Even though globalization has linked all economies, all national economies function in distinctive ways. Every society addresses four basic questions in making decisions that determine how its economy works. The details involved are constantly changing.

How much labor, manufactured capital, and resources from natural capital should be used to produce how much and what kinds of goods and services?

There are three interacting ways of answering this question:

- by markets (voluntary exchange),
- by economic planning by public agencies, corporations, and non-governmental organizations, and
- by unintended side effects of executive, legislative, judicial, or non-governmental decisions made for other reasons.

44

Who owns and profits from Earth's natural capital and society' manufactured and financial capital?

There are four general forms of ownership and profiting:

- Rent from ownership of land-based capital;
- Profit and interest from service and manufacturing based capital;
- Profits from participation in financial markets; and
- Income flows from cooperatives, publicly owned and not-for-profit business.

How is money created and managed?

Three ways, among others, can be distinguished:

- Money is created, and the supply determined, directly by government;
- Money is created when banks make loans in excess of their deposits (fractional reserve banking), and management is overseen by a central bank—the Federal Reserve in the U.S.; and
- Money is created in communities by custom, which is the way it originated, or by design, as is now occurring in many places with the development of local currencies.

How are decisions made about the economy's legal framework and management?

These decisions can be made at different levels, in different ways, and for different purposes:

- At the community, regional, national, or global level;
- By executive, administrative, judicial, legislative or electoral process; and
- Based on priorities involving considerations, such as:
  - o interests of financial investors, producers, employees, and consumers,
  - o differences in taxpayer income, age, and responsibility, and
  - o protection of public health and environmental integrity.

45

By identifying these components and the complexity within them, we unbundle a whole set of considerations that often come wrapped in a single package. At the present time, every nation's government has policies that affect the distribution of income and wealth. Some policies accentuate the tendency for the wealthy to become wealthier. Others moderate this tendency or may even counter-balance it.

We need to apply this understanding to the way economies relate to Earth's overall ecosystem. In small pieces we know how to reduce environmental damage. But overall, governments, international organizations and corporations have not been able to establish a vision of an economy that functions in harmony with nature. The commitment to promoting economic growth in order to create more money and material wealth as an end in itself seems insurmountable.

In a globalized economy, no single nation, local government, organization, or small business could possibly succeed on its own in redesigning its economic activity to function within ecological limits. We tend to think about the economy as illustrated by the Circular Flow diagram.

The Earth is simply missing from this model. All it shows are the markets, as though milk comes from the super market and material goods from some illimitable storehouse. Unbundling the components of an economic system helps to identify many alternatives, which is an essential first step for transforming the system so it can function prosperously within ecological limits.

Money, Banking, and Finance
Ed Dreby and Keith Helmuth

Money was certainly one of humanity's pivotal inventions. Like language, agriculture, architecture, and metallurgy, the use of money and other accepted forms of wealth evolved through practice over time rather than by design. Throughout history, money has existed in many forms, but efforts to understand the nature of money and the way it works have been rather recent. These efforts fall within a range between two contrasting perspectives.

Most economics textbooks state that money and other financial instruments are ethically neutral tools that have evolved to reduce the costs of economic transactions. In this view, money has little effect beyond enabling individuals and communities to meet their needs and wants. Money simply facilitates exchange, so banking and finance must be studied as market phenomena that affect how economies allocate and distribute goods and services, including the ability of one party to use another party's savings.

The other perspective is that money is an integral and influential part of any complex society's economic system. In this view, the form money takes in a particular society has significant ethical and psycho-social effects. The proponents of this perspective hold that systemic features of our monetary and financial structures play a key role in driving indiscriminate economic expansion, intensifying competition, and concentrating income and wealth. They think that re-designing the monetary system would have important and far-reaching social, ethical, and economic effects.

An important question for those concerned with right sharing of Earth's bounty and protecting Earth's life-nurturing capacities is whether today's global monetary system is a significant factor affecting these issues directly, or simply a reflection of other determining factors. Can a more just and ecologically viable society be created using the existing system of money and finance? Are there features of the monetary system that need to be changed in order to make a more just and ecologically viable society possible?

The Value of Money

Money is a social institution based on trust. It can be almost anything that everyone is willing to accept in exchange for everything else. Money serves as a "unit of account" to compare the value of different things, and as a "store of value," which means that people can save it to use later. Within our current monetary system, compound interest makes money a way to accumulate financial wealth.

Commodity money (grain, fur pelts, tobacco, grain, or gold and silver) has useful value in addition to its exchange value. Accumulating commodity money involves accumulating real wealth as well as exchange value.

Token money (paper bills, bank checks, and most modern coinage) only has value as a medium of exchange. Accumulating token money does not accumulate real wealth, only claims to existing or future real wealth. The value of token money depends on people's willingness to use it in exchange for goods and services, and the relationship between the supply of money and the volume of goods and services being exchanged.

Currency (cash) is the form of money currently in use. In today's economies, the most widely used form of money is a national currency: bills and coins printed and minted by the government. Some communities use local currencies in addition to their national currency. National currencies are token money, because the exchange value of paper bills and coinage is unrelated to their value as paper or metal.

Money and Banking

Although governments print the bills and mint the coins, it is the banking system, rather than the government, that creates most of a nation's money supply. A bank creates money when it makes a loan by entering the amount of the loan in a borrower's account as though it is a cash deposit. This enables the borrower to write checks that the bank promises to exchange for cash.

When the borrower pays a third party by a check that is deposited in that party's account, it becomes a new deposit in that party's bank that is no different than if it was a cash deposit. The process by which banks create money is also referred to as "deposit creation." How did this process of creating money out of nothing come about?

Modern banking evolved in 17th century England when the currency was gold. In 1640, King Charles was short of money so he confiscated the gold that some of his subjects had deposited in the

Tower of London. After that, wealthy subjects no longer deposited their gold in the Tower of London, but instead they deposited gold with goldsmiths who had safekeeping vaults.

The goldsmiths gave the depositors receipts for the gold in the form of notes, and paid interest with the understanding they could lend the money out to others. They made these loans by issuing more notes, because it was more convenient for their customers to transact business with the notes rather than the gold itself; so the notes came to serve as money. Only a few depositors redeemed their notes for gold at any one time, so the goldsmiths could easily make loans beyond the value of the gold in their vaults and make a profit for themselves by charging a higher interest rate on the loans than they paid to depositors.

In 1694, King William used the example of the London goldsmiths and chartered the Bank of England to handle royal debt. Wealthy subjects became shareholders and invested money in the Bank. The Bank loaned that money to the King by issuing bank notes. The royal charter allowed the Bank to issue more bank notes as loans to other customers, which meant the gold was loaned twice.

This action by the King made it legal for the Bank to create new money by lending out more than it had on deposit. It meant that the Bank's shareholders could profit both by the interest charged and by the value of the loan when it was repaid. This practice, called *fractional reserve banking,* was gradually extended to other banks and has become the basis of the modern banking industry.

Most¹ nations have created a central bank similar to the Bank of England to manage their national debt and coordinate the private banking system. They have established legal *reserve requirements* specifying the percentage of deposits that bank must hold as a reserve to cover cash withdrawals.

At first the Bank of England's reserve requirement was 50 percent, which meant it could make loans for twice as much as it had in gold deposits. In today's banking systems, the reserve requirements are usually between five and ten percent of a bank's cash deposits, allowing the bank to make loans amounting to 10 to 20 times the amount of money it theoretically possesses. This is why so much of today's money supply is created by banks rather than governments.

Benefits and Risks of
Fractional Reserve Banking

Historically, fractional reserve banking has played a key role, along with science and technology, in creating the advances in health, affluence, and cultural achievements attained by industrialized societies. When banks use new deposits to make loans, and that new money is invested in new productivity, new value is created.

The practice of fractional reserve banking has a *multiplier effect* that makes the supply of money in the system much larger than the amount of currency in circulation. The multiplier effect is the increase of the total money supply as checks and electronic transactions drawn on loans circulate through the economy and back into the banking system as additional deposits. The ability of the money supply to expand as the economy expands has been a major factor in enabling industrial economies to grow and in promoting economic growth.

Most banks require some form of collateral to secure most of their loans. *Collateral* is property pledged as security for the repayment of a loan. Credit cards are a means by which the banking system makes unsecured loans. Before the Great Depression, banks were obligated to redeem their notes in gold or silver coins, but in 1934 the U.S. government ended the domestic gold standard for the dollar, and in 1971, it ended the international gold standard as well. Since then, the value of the dollar has been backed by U.S. government bonds.

In today's system, the creation of money is tied to the creation of either private or public debt, making it a monetary system based on interest-bearing debt. Debt-based money promotes new investment and economic growth as long as borrowers are able to earn enough money to repay their loans with interest. As long as banks re-loan the money when debts are paid, the money supply and the volume of debt is maintained. Banks usually try to do this because it maximizes their profits.

However, the money that borrowers must pay in interest is not created when banks issue a loan. Borrowers must earn the interest they owe from the overall money supply. This means that if all debts are to be paid, there must always be enough increase in the money supply to pay interest on the accumulation of debt. It also means there must always be enough increase in economic activity to sustain the increase in the money supply. Otherwise, some borrowers will have to default. Likewise, under the debt-based monetary system, where the government has given up its sovereign authority to create and control currency, it must tax more than it spends in order to pay interest on its debt.

When a loan is repaid but there is no new loan to replace it, the money created by the original loan will simply disappear from circulation. When loans are not repaid, banks cannot make new loans and must foreclose on mortgages and liquidate collateral (sell the borrowers' properties for currency) in order to meet their obligations to their depositors. The whole system involves not only a multiplier effect when borrowing is increasing, but also a *reverse multiplier effect* when borrowing is decreasing. When borrowing decreases, the money supply is reduced and the circular flows on which commerce and economic prosperity depends are disrupted.

If the economy is expanding, debt holders have a reasonable prospect of increasing their net worth sufficiently to pay interest and still come out ahead. This is the essence of entrepreneurial risk-taking. Difficulties arise if borrowers are unable to repay their loans, if banks are unable to enlarge the aggregate volume of debt, or if there is insufficient increase in economic activity to support the increase of the debt and the money supply.

The Federal Reserve System

As industrialization increased after the U.S. Civil War, banks became increasingly important as a source of financing for farmers, industry, and commerce, but they also contributed to cycles of economic boom and bust. When business was booming, banks were eager to increase their loans. When business slowed, banks became much more cautious about making loans. Thus, when private banks acted in their own best interest, they tended to accentuate instabilities in the economy through the multiplier and reverse multiplier effects on the money supply.

When depositors became afraid a bank would fail, there was a "run" on the bank by its depositors to withdraw their money, which quickly spread to other banks. Bank panics helped create and prolong major economic crises in 1837, 1857, 1873, and 1893. When panics occurred, prices fell, people couldn't pay off their loans, and banks foreclosed on the homes or farms that had secured the loans. There was no coordinated way to prevent banks from failing, so in 1914 the U.S. Congress passed the Federal Reserve Act to establish a central banking system, a development that had already occurred in most other industrialized nations.

The Federal Reserve System (The Fed) was to be an arm of government, isolated from politics, which would serve the public interest by functioning as a bank for the private banks. The Fed would provide for the elasticity of the money supply and the liquidity of the banking system. *Elasticity* refers to the ability of the money supply to expand and contract as needed. *Liquidity* refers to converting assets to currency in order to pay obligations with cash on demand.

The Fed gets its operating funds by a requirement that member banks keep a portion of their reserve requirements on deposit, in return for which they can increase their liquidity by borrowing from the Fed's currency reserves. The Fed also provides a clearinghouse for checks drawn on individual accounts. As a result, personal checks soon replaced bank notes as the banking system's currency.

Great Depression and Banking Reforms

Until 1934, the U.S. money supply was backed by gold. This only worked well if the growth of the economy was paralleled by an increase in the gold supply, which was the case for most of the 19th century. But as economic growth increased during the 20th century, international trade and finance heavily affected the gold supply. The increase in the gold supply could not keep pace with the speculative stock market boom of the 1920s.

The Federal Reserve System was intended to provide emergency liquidity for individual banks, but with an enlarged economic system and a huge speculative bubble backed by a limited supply of gold, there was little the Fed could do to prevent a run on the whole system when the stock market crashed in 1929. Bank failures during the Great Depression led the government to eliminate the gold standard as the basis for the nation's currency, create the Federal Deposit Insurance Corporation, and prevent commercial banks from participating in the financial markets.

Monetary Policy

A more fundamental result of the Great Depression was the analysis of its causes by John Maynard Keynes and like-minded economists, Keynesians. They argued that monetary policy should be used in conjunction with fiscal policy (government spending and taxation) to moderate, and at times counteract, the cyclical tendencies of economic activity to expand or contract. Monetary policy refers to the tools available to the Fed for managing the money supply:

- *open market operations*, the buying and selling of government bonds;

- changing the *interest rate* the Fed charges on loans to member banks;

- changing the *reserve requirement*, the fraction of a bank's total deposits legally required to keep on deposit with the Fed and as cash deposits in the bank itself; and

- *adding money directly* into the economy.

By buying or selling bonds the Fed decreases or increases its own cash reserves, thereby increasing or decreasing the currency in circulation. Open market operations are the least intrusive of its tools, so buying or selling bonds is the Fed's predominant means of managing the money supply. By changing the interest rate on its loans to member banks, the Fed invites or discourages individual banks to borrow from the Fed to increase their loans to customers. By changing the reserve requirement the Fed can alter the dynamic of the multiplier effect in the entire banking system. This has a drastic effect on the economy, but the most drastic is adding money directly into the economy.

The Fed's basic purpose is to provide monetary stability. In the 1920s and 1930s, bitter experience taught that drastic action usually made things worse. Yet in the 2008 crisis, the Fed took drastic action and added money directly into the economy, because so much money had disappeared as the financial markets contracted.

Post-World War II Era

At the end of World War II, the U.S. had an intact industrial capacity and huge gold reserves that had been received in payment for supplying the wartime needs of other nations. Under the 1944 Bretton Woods agreements, the U.S. dollar became the currency of international trade backed by U.S. gold reserves, based on an international exchange rate of $35 per ounce of gold. All other currencies were valued in relationship to the U.S. dollar.

The Fed then managed the U.S. money supply for over 20 years according to Keynesian monetary theories. The central banks of other nations used similar tools to manage their money supplies in order to maintain the value of their currencies in relation to the U.S. dollar. The effect was global monetary stability.

During the 1950s, Keynesians wanted to use fiscal policy to promote economic growth. At that time fiscal conservatives were opposed to government policies to promote growth because they thought too much growth might destabilize the monetary system and create another depression. This was one of the policy issues debated in the Kennedy-Nixon presidential election.

Keynesian monetary and fiscal policy seemed to work well until the late 1960s when dollars began accumulating outside the U.S. and could theoretically be redeemed for the limited supply of gold. The U.S. Treasury faced a series of crises in the form of possible runs on the U.S. gold supply. In 1971, the Nixon administration decreed that it would no longer exchange dollars for gold, which finally put an end to the gold standard in relation to the value of the dollar.

Global Financial Architecture

Since 1971, all national currencies have had their relative values determined by global currency exchange markets. The global money supply is no longer tied to any real commodity. This has allowed the global money supply to expand to keep pace with the expansion of the global economy. However, it has also diminished the ability of national central banks, like the Fed, to manage domestic money supplies. As a result, central banks and international monetary institutions have been challenged to work cooperatively to develop a global monetary policy, a challenge not yet met in practice because large, private, global banks have effectively freed themselves from central banking control.

The monetary challenges facing the global community have been exacerbated by the following recent trends:

- Innovations in computing and electronic communication have increased the ease with which virtually any financial investment can be exchanged for currency, blurring the distinction between money and other financial assets;

- Restrictions on financial transfers between countries have been eased;

54

- The U.S. has eliminated many of the legal distinctions between banks and other financial services corporations;

- Research in the mathematics of finance has yielded a host of new financial instruments that may be derived from a single source of expected income. Using mathematical formulas to define the relationship among options, futures, and various derivative products tends to amplify the impact of changes in one financial market on another; and

- Powerful computers enable traders to exploit even tiny arbitrage opportunities for substantial gain. *Arbitrage* is the purchasing of securities on one market and reselling on another where the valuation is slightly higher.

In 1970 the dollar value of annual U.S. financial transactions was about twice the dollar value of the real economy (the goods and services economy). By the 1990s the financial economy had grown to between 20 and 50 times the size of the real economy and has continued to increase since then. The increased volume and liquidity of global financial instruments have been persistent destabilizing forces. Sudden "capital flight" has led to macro-economic and foreign exchange crises involving Mexico, Russia, Argentina, and the leading South Asian economies in the 1990s. In 1999, the U.S. law preventing commercial banks from participating in the financial markets was eliminated, which added to the opportunities for financial speculation by an array of financial institutions that had previously been limited in their activities.

The global money supply that was estimated to be about $2 trillion in 1970, grew from about $25 trillion in 2000 to a peak of over $60 trillion by the summer of 2008 (*Figure 3, p. 56*). Because the economy will contract if it doesn't keep expanding, one wonders whether all the abuses that took place precipitated the great unraveling of 2008, or kept it from happening sooner than it did.

A Monetary System Based on Interest-bearing Debt

The failure of the financial system in 2008-2009 underscores the intrinsic perils of a debt-based monetary system controlled and operated by private for-profit banks and associated financial institutions that have grown "too big to fail." As this pamphlet goes to press, the global financial system seems to be in a condition of permanent crisis, and there is no satisfactory resolution in sight.

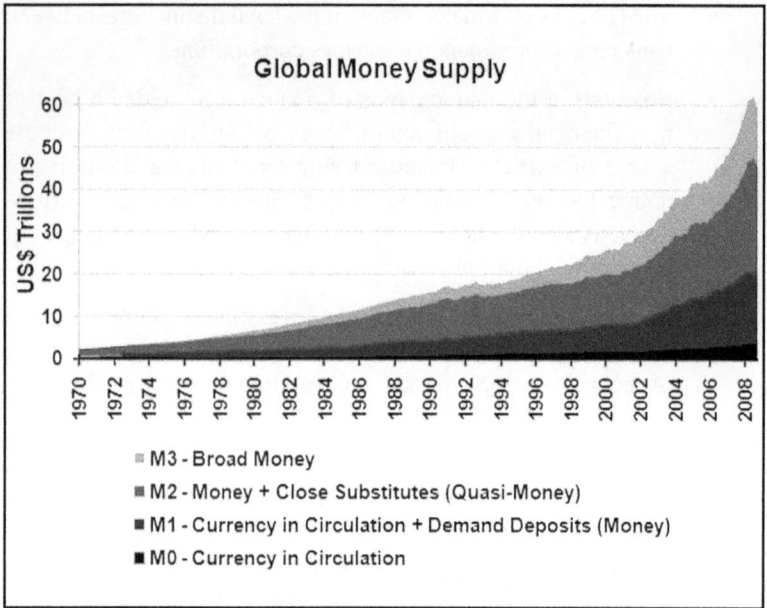

Figure 3. Gobal Money Supply <dollardaze.org>

There is also no resolution about the implications of money, banking and the global financial system for the ecological integrity of our planet. Some policy professionals argue that the system necessarily demands ever more exploitation of a finite and already stressed biosphere. Others see promise in harnessing global markets to share the costs of environmental protection and restoration. Some see a need for modest reforms, along the lines creating a global equivalent to the U.S. Federal Reserve. Others see a need for fundamental changes in the design and functioning of the entire global monetary system.

One of the questions Kenneth Boulding asked was how changes in the proportion of aggregate income coming from interest, profits, and wages would affect the rate of unemployment. He observed that when the percentage of interest income was high relative to profits, especially as in the 1930s, employment was low, whether or not wages were high. When the percentage of interest income was low relative to profits, employment tended to be high. He also observed that, while income from interest was about one percent of national income in the 1950s, by the 1980s interest income had grown to about ten percent of national income. He suggested that considering the causes and effects of this shift was apt to be important for understanding many other changes occurring in U.S. and global economies.

In an "empty" world there are many opportunities to increase the economic throughput of markets so that everyone can become wealthier. A debt-based monetary system enhances these opportunities by creating financial capital to promote economic development and by enabling the money supply to expand as debt and throughput expands. As the world becomes "full," the pressures increase to incorporate ever more resources and human economic activity into the market system so that borrowers can pay interest and still come out ahead. If the economy is not expanding, the effect of interest-bearing debt is to transfer wealth, or claims on future wealth, from borrowers to lenders, that is, from the less wealthy to the wealthier.

The current debt-based monetary system as it has evolved over the past century would appear to be only one option within an array of other possibilities. The U.S. government successfully issued debt-free greenbacks during and after the Civil war. The U.S. Treasury was still issuing debt-free money as recently as 1971. The Bank of Canada created and managed debt-free money from 1935 to 1974. Many communities throughout the world are successfully using local currencies that are issued without debt.

As the world becomes more crowded one important question is: How can the current debt-based monetary system be adapted to serve the needs of a "spaceship economy" in which economic throughput is restrained so it remains within the productive and assimilative capacities of the biosphere?

As with other challenges we face, resolving long-term questions about the adaptabilities of the monetary system need not prevent us from supporting near-term policy actions around which agreement is more likely to be found, such as:

- debt relief for the poorest nations and regions;
- strategies for directing a fair share of societal wealth and windfall financial returns to the common good;
- strategies for establishing a basic living income for all citizens;
- global "circuit breakers" to prevent panic selling on global financial exchanges; and
- ways to ensure that financial flows accurately reflect the costs of environmental harms associated with specific economic activities.

CHAPTER THREE

Ethics and Economic Theory

Leonard Joy

Modern economic theory is the rationale for contemporary capitalism. While it purports to be ethically neutral, it is underpinned by a profoundly antisocial ethic and an immature values system. The values of the Religious Society of Friends—and the similar values of many other religious traditions—express how we relate to ourselves, to other humans, to all of Earth's life systems, and the cosmos. Economists largely ignore these relationships in the application of economic theory, which makes economics at base amoral and, in practice, often immoral.

By assuming that human goals are expressed as the maximization of the market value of production, the prevailing economic theory fails to account for who bears the costs and who reaps the benefits, which generates poverty as it promotes material abundance. Our current economic system also fails to account for the impacts on living systems, so economic growth is pursued regardless of the consequences to the natural capital that sustains it. By disregarding both nature and persons, the fundamentalist application of economic theory violates not only Quaker testimonies, but also the ethical teachings of all world religions on social relations. Today, this lack of regard threatens life itself.

Development of Modern Economic Theory

Economics originated as a branch of philosophy concerned with the attainment of the "good life," especially through the husbandry of resources. As national economic systems developed, the field of economics became concerned, not only with the creation of wealth, but also with the distribution of wealth and the systematic management of economic activity. Under the influence of 19th century scientism there were attempts to express the economic system—the relations among production, consumption, prices, savings, investment, wages, and incomes—mathematically. The mathematicians built impressive models and a comprehensive mathematical framework emerged for the analysis of economic systems.

This framework gave new and powerful, though narrow, insights into how economic variables were related. However, it was based on several simplifying assumptions that were unsupported by empirical observation. Economists accepted these simplifying abstractions as valid approximations of reality even though the limitations of the analysis, the unreality of its assumptions, and serious challenges to the validity of its conclusions were profoundly apparent.

Not the least consequence of these simplifying abstractions was that they avoided consideration of social justice concerns that had been at the core of 19th century economics debates. This resulted in the notion that concerns about economic exploitation, for example, were groundless because whatever wages resulted from a perfect market were inevitably fair. They represented the true value of labor to the producer and they were the best wages that laborers could properly find, claim, and justify.

In the middle of the Great Depression, English Economist Lionel Robbins[33] provided what became widely accepted as the justification for modern economics' silence on social justice issues. He argued that economics did not depend upon value judgments and that it had nothing to say about them. He thereby both rationalized the exclusion of social justice from the subject matter of economics, and ignored the underlying value premises on which its theories are based.

According to Robbins, the role of the economist was not to pronounce on social values, but to accept the values of society. The economist's job was making calculations to determine optimum allocation of resources for pursuing desired socio-political goals that were determined outside the science of economics. The agenda of the political economists—Ricardo, Marx, and others—to create a just and prosperous society, was thereby discarded as outside the scope of economics.

This view was supported by another English Economist, John Hicks,[34] who purported to show that optimum resource allocation (the distribution of goods and services among consumers that would maximize everyone's satisfaction) could be determined without knowing just how much satisfaction was derived from any specific outcome. All that was needed was to assume that individuals had a consistent rank ordering of preferences. Hicks asserted that this was adequate not only for the understanding of individual choice, but as a basis for advocacy with regard to the social good.

Robbins had argued that the professional task of the economist was to present the economic and material consequences of alternate choices and allow society to choose. This effectively removed economists altogether from the advocacy of specific social policy. By applying the work of Hicks and others, some economists concluded that they could and should advocate for the promotion of free markets as the means of best expressing the social good, thereby eliminating the need for society to choose societal goals. This conclusion stemmed from the theoretical demonstration that, when in equilibrium, the market could be shown to produce a pattern of production and consumption that was optimal in terms of the sum and distribution of everyone's individual level of satisfaction. This in turn was seen as the objectively desirable social goal.

The practical application of this theorizing required rigorous and unrealistic assumptions, including:

- The market is perfect with no monopolies, and with no barrier to information or the movement of goods and resources, including labor; and

- The distribution of income and wealth created by markets is ideal.

These limitations of economic theory and its application have been played down and ignored by the advocates of privatization and free markets.

Economic Theory Denies Earth

One basic reality that is unaccounted for by current applications of economic theory is the limit to the capacity of global environment to indefinitely meet demands upon it. The current theoretical assumption that continued growth is both necessary and possible is inconsistent with the limit of the finite world on which we live. The practical applications of current theory do not reflect concerns about the health of the global natural and social environments that sustain us. There is no accounting in our economic system for the costs of natural resources of Earth that are being exploited in current energy production, manufacturing, and transportation.

Free Market Economics
Excludes the Common Good

The theoretical framework from which this free market advocacy was derived excludes the concept of the common good by the assumption that all individual wants are independent. There is no need for social goals because they have been assumed not to exist. Thus, there is no need for a government to concern itself, for example, with the health of individuals. What it needs to concern itself with is the creation of a free market in health services.

Many economists have adapted to find a new role in this situation. They might argue that if society, through a political process decides to support people whose incomes are so low they cannot afford to buy health services in this free market, then it may be desirable to supplement their incomes so they can afford these services. Economic theory could then suggest ways of redistributing income that might do the least damage to the efficient working of the market.

Eliminating the concept of the common good in economic theory is profoundly significant in shaping contemporary society because this omission allows us to ignore how economic policies have a major influence on the way we relate to one another. It isn't simply the economist's denial of the existence of a common good and dismissal of concerns for relationships and community that is so corrosive to society. There has also been a triumphant marriage of the amoral economist and libertarian philosopher that reinforces the denial of the need for common social values and purpose.

While free market economists espouse maximizing self-interest and freedom to trade in markets, libertarians espouse minimum constraint on the freedom of expression. These beliefs are grounded in the assumption of economic theory that if each person pursues his or her own tastes and values, and each seeks self-interested material gain by joining competing coalitions, the greatest social good will result. This leads both free market economists and libertarians to argue vehemently for individual freedom and against collective action for the common good.

Thus, economic theory that claims to be objective is used to support the conclusion that free markets are preferable to social governance through the articulation and pursuit of shared social goals. Given a free market and perfect competition, social problems are seen to arise only because consumers and voters are not fully informed and therefore do not understand their true self-interest. It is argued, therefore, that, in the service of the free market, assuring transparency (public access to information) and preventing monopoly power are legitimate and important public policy goals. In addition, it is regarded as necessary to invoke legal sanctions when one party's pursuit of self-interest causes harm to another party or parties. Otherwise, free market theory assumes people and corporations should be free to do whatever is in their own best interest and not against the law.

Alternative Paradigms

Yet, this values system is not the only possible basis for economic theory. There are alternative paradigms that would answer the legitimate questions asked of the current paradigm, and address questions that should be asked—questions about justice and the pursuit of the good life that economics embarked on centuries ago. Ethics and religion are about relationship. Meaning and values are about relationships. The economy is a domain of relationships. Economic theories that deny the significance of relationship, that reflect immature values, that embody no sense of social development other than simple growth, are not adequate for advancing the good of the whole society within a healthy environment.

Simplicity Is Not Enough: Structural Violence and the Peace Testimony

Margaret Mansfield and Ed Dreby

Friends have a longstanding commitment to non-violence, and to relieve the suffering caused by war or other forms of direct violence. In seeking to be faithful to the Peace Testimony, we are also called to discover the seeds of war around and within us.

Many Friends see the Testimony on Simplicity as a key to addressing the seeds of violence in their lives. They understand that high levels of material consumption create economic demand that accelerates the exploitation of people and the planet. However, the current economic system must either expand or contract. If consumption were significantly reduced the economy would contract, leading to more unemployment, malnutrition and poverty. Moreover, even when our consumer-based economy is expanding, it systematically causes physical and psychic harm to millions of people.

Norwegian Sociologist Johan Galtung first developed the concept of structural violence in 1969.[35] By the 1980s, the harmful effects of "structural adjustment programs" imposed by the International Monetary Fund on debtor nations led a number of humanitarians, including some Quakers, to describe the IMF's oppressive economic policies as "structural violence."

Structural violence occurs when physical and psychic harm results from the conduct of social institutions stemming from laws, regulations, and policies, rather than being directly caused by overt force.

For example, in 1990 the International Monetary Fund required the government of Peru to privatize publicly owned assets and services as a condition of preventing a financial crisis. Within days its implementation led to extreme food shortages and price increases of more than 500 percent. By 1991, only five percent of Lima's workforce was fully employed and over half of Peru's population lacked enough income to meet basic needs.[36]

Each year far more people die from hunger-related diseases than from war and other forms of human physical violence, even though enough food is produced globally for everyone to have enough to eat. Economic exploitation and institutional indifference to chronic hunger and treatable diseases systematically violates the basic right of people everywhere to the opportunity for healthy, useful, and spiritually rewarding lives. This, too, is structural violence.

Characteristics of Structural Violence

Sociologist Susan James describes structural violence as "nested within three systems—the socio-political, the socio-environmental, and the psychological." The economic system intersects in innumerable ways with our society's social psychology and its effects on our politics and environmental impacts. Her analysis suggests that structural violence has four major characteristics.[37]

Structural violence is **hidden** because it is embedded in the distant institutions that govern our lives. With economic globalization, what happens in distant financial markets can have devastating effects on vulnerable people and communities. For example, in 2005 financial speculators began to shift from housing to farm commodities futures. By 2008 the prices of corn, rice and wheat had nearly tripled, resulting in a worldwide food crisis of increased hunger, food riots, and civil unrest (*Figure 4*). Rising oil prices, unfavorable weather and the market for biofuels were contributing factors, but financial speculation made the markets more volatile, and turned a bad situation into a worldwide crisis, resulting in millions more malnourished people.[38]

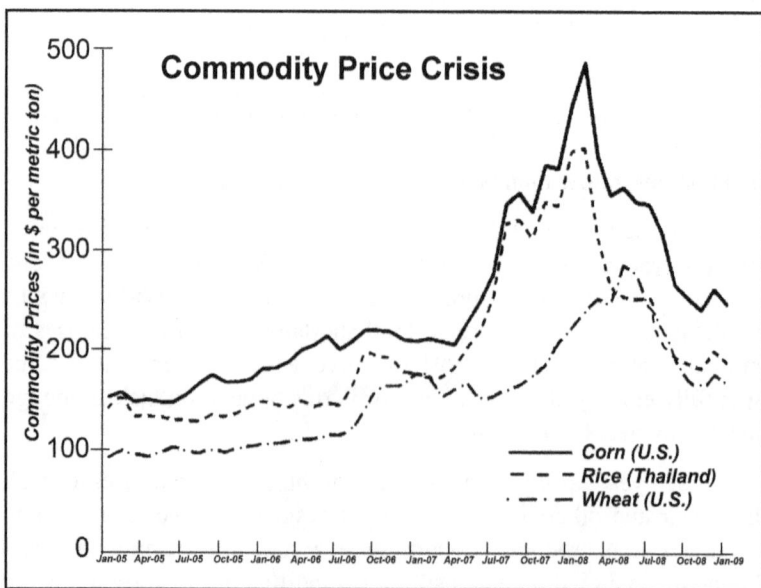

Figure 4. Commodity Price Crisis (Food and Water Watch, 2009)

Structural violence is also hidden because it leads people to do harmful things for what seem to be good reasons. Most people who make and carry out harmful policy decisions are not motivated by malice. They are simply doing their job. The 2008 housing crisis in the U.S. offers an example, where TV news showed sheriff's deputies evicting people from their homes, and carpenters boarding them up. Both were unhappily doing their jobs and neither had anything to do with the speculation and corruption that led to the housing and foreclosure crisis.

Structural violence is **shortsighted** in the sense that it damages everyone, including future generations. Just as John Woolman revealed to Quaker slave masters the ways slavery embroils master and slave alike in relationships that violate Gospel Order,[39] so, too, do the economic policies that keep Americans addicted to fossil fuels today. Oil subsidies and regulatory exemptions like the "Halliburton Loophole" enable dangerous and destructive energy production like deep sea drilling and hydraulic fracking.[40] While highly lucrative for a few, such policies are shortsighted not only because they promote short-term profits over long-term solutions but also because they embroil everyone in a web of daily activities that damage future generations, hamper innovation and burden the Spirit.

Structural violence is **self-reinforcing**. In many conditions of poverty, interrelated deprivations of inadequate nutrition, health care, education, and economic opportunity, create a vicious cycle from which few can escape within the given rules. Once known for its electronics and food industries, Camden, New Jersey, is now among the poorest cities in the nation with a population that is 85 percent African American and Hispanic. Nearly one quarter of its citizens live on less than $10,000 a year without adequate primary health care and housing. The high concentration of low-income people in Camden City reflects the *de facto* segregation within Camden County, the median income of which is three times higher than that of the city. Children in Cambden City are at far higher risk of stunted physical and intellectual development from chronic malnutrition, lead poisoning, underfunded public schools, playgrounds and libraries, and the ever-present danger of street violence.[41]

Finally, structural violence **promotes scapegoating**. When people blame the victims or the agents of action leading to violence, they divert attention from its underlying causes. The insinuation that people are poor because they are lazy, ignorant, or immoral underlies much of the rhetoric that opposes social welfare programs. Following September 11, 2001, a wave of fear targeted Muslims as potential threats. This was used to justify intrusive laws that erode civil liberties for Arab Americans and other immigrants and has undermined our nation's spiritual values and ethical standards. It also deflects attention from the ways in which our nation's foreign policies are causing structural as well as physical violence to Muslim societies.

Structural Economic Violence

In a market economy, legal systems give priority to protecting property rights over meeting basic human needs. As economies become increasingly monetized, the focus of access to life's necessities shifts from localities and households to national markets and global corporations, and having money becomes essential to physical and psychic wellbeing. Consumer culture teaches us to seek happiness in the accumulation of material goods. This distances us from one another and isolates vulnerable people. The ways money is acquired and spent help make clear how structural economic violence is inflicted on the poor.

Modern corporations inflict structural violence through a variety of profit-driven strategies. Downsizing, indifference to and abuses of employees, use of temp agencies and prison labor, and abandonment of the communities that helped them grow are among the most common practices. The prevalence of U.S. industrial toxic contamination in minority communities and the complicity of regulatory agencies constitutes a form of "environmental racism" where white power and privilege disadvantage people of color.

A classic example of environmental racism is the case of Warren County, North Carolina. In 1978 a waste-hauling company drove tanker trucks through state roads in rural North Carolina with open valves letting out PCB-laden liquid waste from Ward Transformer Company, contaminating the shoulders of 240 miles of roads. The perpetrators were prosecuted and the state of North Carolina's solution was to construct a landfill in Warren County to accommodate 40,000 cubic yards of contaminated road shoulder soil. Since it was clear that the site was chosen because majority of residents of Warren County were African-American and poor, a protest against the landfill attracted the attention of regional and national civil rights leaders and effectively began the environmental racism movement.[42] Sociologist Robert Bullard clearly demonstrates that hazardous waste sites are often sited

66

in minority communities where environmental regulations remain unenforced (*Figure 5*).[43]

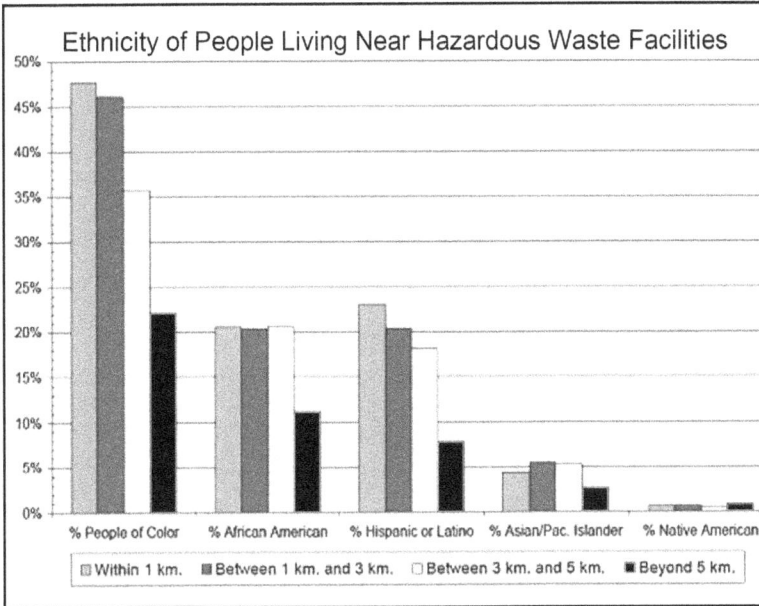

Figure 5. Ethnicity of People Living Near Hazardous Waste Facilities (Bullard, *et al*, 2007)

The immorality of some major industrial corporations has been joined by the immorality of the elites of the financial sector, who acquired immense fortunes by devising means and securing legislation to manufacture profit from widespread predatory lending, and who used inscrutable financial instruments to defraud their customers, stockholders, the federal government, and ultimately the entire nation in the financial crisis of 2008.

Structural Violence from an Ecological Perspective

The concept of structural violence has been developed primarily by advocates for social and economic justice. But the same considerations apply to the human-Earth relationship. Systematic damage to Earth's life-sustaining cycles through human–induced disasters is also structural violence. Just as the inequitable distribution of wealth constitutes structural violence when it deprives people of basic needs; so, too, does degrading the soils and destabilizing the climate. The prospects for future generations are likewise diminished as aquifers are depleted, arable lands turned into deserts, and limited material resources exhausted by the current systems of exploitation.

Quakers and Structural Violence: Why Simplicity is Not Enough

Structural violence as a concept is of recent origin. Yet, many of the social causes for which notable Friends provided leadership were responses to instances of structural violence of an earlier time. In the past, the abolition of slavery, prison reform, women's rights, and other crusades for justice have been viewed as separate from the Friends Peace Testimony. As the idea of structural violence becomes more widespread among Friends, it may become yet another way the Peace Testimony has evolved from its 17th century origins to today's broader, yet perhaps more controversial, applications.

The Testimony on Simplicity is important, both as a spiritual exercise and as an element in addressing problems of structural economic violence. Yet people make choices in the context of a system. Without intention or design, institutional structures limit our spiritual, ethical, and practical choices. Understanding the dysfunctional aspects of these systems and helping to change them are as essential as faithfully living our Testimony of Simplicity. When Friends come to see all our testimonies as parts of a complex whole, we will more clearly see the violence embedded in our economic, social, and political institutions. Thus we can begin to move closer to a world at peace through justice, where everyone has adequate access to the means of life and life development resources.

Must Poverty Always Be With Us?
George Lakey[44]

In the U.S. there is a widespread assumption among people of goodwill, that poverty is a given, a necessary dimension of the human condition. Sometimes people will quote from the Bible, "the poor will always be with you." This assumption is in articles about justice and social change and in the tone of despair in the voices of people who are socially concerned. However, poverty can be virtually abolished, and there are countries that have already done just that.

The Norway Example

At the beginning of the 20th century Norway was a very poor country with most people living in slums or rural poverty. There were small groups of rich owners and middle class people. Most Norwegians were workers and farmers. The income difference between the rich and the poor was dramatic. But there were some who had a vision of greater equality. A small number of Norwegian Quakers, first established in 1814, promoted the testimony of equality. Over the 19th and into the 20th century a larger movement for social justice came into action. In Norway, an alliance that included workers, farmers, and some middle-class people became the political majority and took democratic control of the government. But it was not easy. The workers, farmers, and their allies mobilized a large-scale, non-violent struggle to change political and economic control. Wave after wave of large public demonstrations, strikes, and boycotts made the country ungovernable. The owning class government called out the troops and tried to violently suppress the demands for change. It was not pretty. People were hurt and killed, but government violence failed, and political change came to Norway that has set the course of its development ever since. [45]

Norway and other Scandinavian countries made a choice to eliminate poverty. Norway abolished slums and put its population into good housing, gave everyone good health care and a secure retirement, and provided free university education. And they did all that before the North Sea oil was discovered. Norway pretty much gave up poverty while it still had fewer resources per capita than does the U.S.

How did they do it? They created a national goal with a national strategy, which included:

Universal services instead of services linked to income.
The success of Norway in eliminating poverty, and the abject failure of fabulously wealthy countries like the U.S. to do so, has led some scholars to conclude; "Programs for the poor are poor programs." Based on results, only universal services hold the promise of eliminating poverty. Take the U.S. health care system, for example, through which Americans pay twice as much per capita for health care and still leave tens of millions uninsured and countless of the insured locked into worry and inadequate care.

Prioritize education and training. Norway places the highest value on the development of people. This begins with extended maternity and paternity leave and universal day care for children. In Norway, education is a basic, publicly supported service available to all from childhood through university and graduate school. If a student wants to study medicine but Norway doesn't have enough spaces, the system pays for the student to study and be trained abroad. Various subsidies and interest free loans for living expenses and educational supplies are available for students that need extra assistance. Norway provides full support for mentally challenged and differently abled people.

Make cultural and artistic assets central. Norway provides state support for theatre, dance, opera, music groups, symphony orchestras, grass-roots arts groups, and for agencies that distribute arts and culture programs to remote areas. The flourishing film industry is also subsidized.

Use taxation as a flexible means of distributing wealth and eliminating poverty. Norway once, like the U.S., had a very big range of incomes, from the very rich to the very poor. Norwegians strategically reduced that range on both ends, producing a range that moves toward social equality. Norway uses a steeply graduated income tax but everyone ends up paying a lot of their income in taxes one way or another, and that is how they want it. Prime Minister Jens Stoltenberg said, "We won two elections promising not to lower taxes." The most frequent attitude of Norwegians is, "To get a lot, we pay a lot." The result is an extraordinarily high level of trust among Norwegian citizens that things will work. The payoff for the economy includes high productivity, a minimum of "me-first" behavior, conscientious monitoring and elimination of waste and inefficiency, low corruption and cheating, and continual public debate about the future direction of the economy as a whole.

Make the economy serve the people's values instead of the other way round. Norway has developed an economy with public majority share ownership in major corporations and with a large sector of cooperatively owned and operated businesses. Credit Unions (co-op banks) and state banks regulate and manage the credit system for maximum social benefit. Various levels of government, including municipal and local, carefully supervise land use and environmental impact. Public policy and public support is targeted to keep agricultural and fishing communities attractive and viable for young people and families.

Placing the well-being of people and communities at the center of national development became possible when the domination of the economy by a rich Norwegian elite was abolished. This political change was accomplished in the 1930s. All the structural and policy changes that set Norway on its path to prosperity and equity were accomplished before the windfall of North Sea oil. The other Scandinavian countries have followed a similar course of social and economic development without the benefit of oil money.

Norway's handling of North Sea oil is instructive. After national discussion, it was decided that:

- the oil would be owned by the people as a whole through a state corporation, rather than to privatize it,

- the oil would be extracted gradually to extend its benefits for many generations,

- oil companies like Exxon would be contracted to work for Norway only for as long as it took to teach Norwegians the technology,

- oil workers would be unionized,

- cities like Stavanger near oil fields would not suffer boom and bust cycles but would have controlled growth, and

- the benefit of the oil income would be for all the people.

This remarkable set of policies was possible because Norwegian capitalists are not allowed to dominate economic decision-making. Norway has not given up capitalism. It has retained the function of markets and their benefits within an economy that operates first and foremost for the well-being of people.

The Iceland example

Traditionally, Iceland was in worse shape than Norway. A majority of people in Iceland lived in poverty for centuries. Iceland then virtually abolished poverty, using a strategy like Norway's. Central to its strategy was not waiting until wealth was created to set up universal services, but to institute services as part of economic development. Iceland found that a healthier population was also a more economically productive population.

What about the recent collapse of Iceland's financial system? Icelandic banks, having been tempted into joining the international speculation bubble, caused the 2007-2008 collapse of Iceland's financial system. The country temporarily forgot how dangerous unregulated markets can be. Iceland was rescued by strong government action that allowed failed banks to fail, making international creditors take the fall instead of bailing them out at taxpayer expense. In making this move, the Icelandic government protected the country's basic services and is now widely acclaimed as having done the right thing. Norway and Sweden made similar moves toward bank nationalization a few years earlier when they could see what was coming if the industry was allowed to continue its high-risk behavior. The Scandinavian flirtation with neo-liberal deregulation was short-lived. Norway and Sweden forestalled the financial collapse that hit Iceland, Ireland, UK, U.S., etc.[46]

What About Trade and Globalization?

Global economic integration is said to be the inevitable course of history, so we might expect that Norway would figure prominently in the development of the European Common Market. Remarkably, Norway refuses to join the European Union. The leadership of all major political parties, even Labour, wanted to join many years ago, but a massive social movement arose that forced a referendum in which the Norwegians rejected EU membership, fearing that their ability to democratically steer their own economy would be lost to the global giants. In a world where even large nations bow humbly to the will of international financiers, little Norway, a nation of 4 million people, is still in charge of its own economy.

Summary

Sometimes people feel discouraged about the chances of human beings ever developing a society without harsh class divisions. The case of Norway suggests that class, as we know it in the U.S., is not hardwired into the human species.

Norwegians are among those with the highest living standard in the world, and not because of North Sea oil. Before the oil was discovered, Norway

- virtually abolished poverty as a matter of national policy,

- eliminated slums and provided good housing for all,

- provided free education plus a living stipend for students,

- provided an excellent national health care system that covered everyone regardless of income,

- subsidized quality mass public transport to reduce the strain on the environment and make transit easy,

- strongly subsidized major art institutions as well as grassroots and startup initiatives,

- became one of the top countries in the world in per capita giving to development in the Global South, and

- provided excellent care for seniors, with adequate guaranteed income, care at home or retirement communities with nursing facilities.

The result is a society far more democratic than the U.S., without the economic chokehold of state socialism or the anxiety and human wastage of unfettered market fundamentalism, and with far more opportunity for individuals to do what they feel called to do, except to exploit their neighbor. Norway is not a classless society, nor is it without a continuing struggle to achieve a better balance of fairness in economic and social life, but it does show that human beings do not have to live the way we do in the U.S.

Cooperatives: An Alternative to Profit-Driven Corporations

Ed Snyder

One of Quakerism's highest values regarding the wider community involves maximum participation and widely shared power.[47]

The philosophy of the democratic state, in particular, grows out of the same roots as the Quaker faith. Basic to each is the belief in the sacredness of the individual and the conviction that each person may contribute something of worth.[48]

In the *political* arena, democracy, with all its warts and shortcomings, has the potential to come the closest to Friends' ideals of respecting the innate worth and talents of each individual.

Every opportunity for participation in decisions of public matters by ballot should be used. When exercising their duties as individual voters, Friends are urged to make careful study of public questions, avoid opinionated arguments, maintain a clearness of judgment which will enable them to act upon principle, and support what they believe to be sound policies."[49]

In the *economic* sphere we are far from this ideal. In contrast with the political arena where the stated goal is "one person, one vote," and each individual's vote is important, the economic arena is dominated by an *authoritarian* model, via corporations. Corporate decisions are made by managers whose main responsibility is to the economic welfare of the shareholders of their particular corporation.

Friends, in their relations with corporations, whether as stockholders or otherwise, should be governed by the same high standards as in their relations with individuals. If the conduct of a corporation is inconsistent with high standards of individual conduct, it should be the duty of Friends, if protests do not avail, to refuse to retain ownership of the stock, or be the recipient of income in any form from such a corporation.[50]

U.S. history is replete with stories of the "robber barons," rapacious corporations that disregarded workers' rights, community values, and the environment. Corporations have used their wealth to dominate the political life of our nation through campaign contributions, paid lobbyists and ill-concealed bribery, buying control of legislatures and the executive and judicial branches in many areas of federal and state government. Two eras of reform, one at the turn of the 20th century, and one following the Great Depression of the 1930's resulted in the citizenry working through their government to break up the monopolies, support workers' rights, and protect the public health and welfare. But today we are in full retreat from these goals, as we see the dysfunction and virtual paralysis of our federal government, and the Supreme Court declaring that corporations are persons. Today, it is fair to say we are a plutocracy—government by the wealthy—not a republic or democracy.

Are there ways that individual citizens can have an impact in the economic arena? One of the few effective ways we have is to vote with the dollars we spend. Today, the markets where we shop are carrying more local products, more organic food, and more fair trade, worker produced items. There is no doubt this is in response to consumer demand. But regrettably, the number of people who use their purchasing power in this way is far too small to have a major influence on the role of corporations in our economy. Why? One reason is price. Such products often cost more, and there are many poor consumers who, out of necessity, buy goods at the lowest price in order to make their meager dollars go further. Another reason is corporate advertising that downplays the costs of poor nutrition, environmental damage, pollution caused by their products and other "externalities;" and they cleverly manipulate consumer information to their advantage.

Cooperatives—A Best-kept Secret

There is an alternative to the autocratic corporate model that provides a democratic way to make decisions on economic issues—the cooperative. According to one definition by the United Nations Indigenous Youth Council, "Co-operatives, or co-ops, are a type of business characterized by democratic ownership and governance. They offer an alternative to the shareholder model of business ownership. Co-ops are governed by their members, who typically invest in the co-operative and have an ownership stake in it, as well as a voice in how the firm is run. Decisions are often made on a one-member, one-vote basis; so in many societies, co-ops provide a much-needed example of democratic governance amid otherwise inequitable conditions." Cooperatives have a great potential+ to replace corporations in our economic system.

In the United States: Currently there are nearly 30,000 cooperatives operating at 73,000 places of business throughout the U.S.

Most are found in agriculture, farm credit, federal home loans, food stores and rural electricity. They have more than three trillion dollars in assets, account for more than two million jobs and pay more than $75 billion in wages and benefits. Most citizens have an opportunity to be a part of this process by depositing money in a nearby credit union where they have access to all banking services and often lower cost mortgage loans than are available at banks. They can also participate in decision-making and share in any profits generated by the enterprise. Credit unions escaped much of the financial meltdown disaster of 2008 because they had not sold their mortgages to larger entities as many commercial banks did.

Why is so little known about the value of cooperatives in the U.S.? Does the corporate world deliberately downplay their importance? Interestingly, the University of Wisconsin Center for Cooperatives, from which many of the figures in the preceding paragraph are taken, reports the following on its website:

> Given the unique niche that cooperatives fill in the U.S. economy, it is unfortunate that so little is known about where and how cooperatives operate. Unlike data-reporting agencies of many other countries, the U.S. Census Bureau does not identify cooperatives in any of its census or business reporting surveys. As a consequence, there are no federally reported data on cooperatives in the United States. The purpose of this project is to fill this gap by conducting a census of cooperatives, and by measuring their impact on aggregate income and employment.[51]

Around the World: Cooperatives are a worldwide phenomena, more widely used as an economic model than in the U.S. Indeed the United Nations in 2012 is currently in the middle of the International Year of Cooperatives "intended to raise public awareness of the invaluable contributions of cooperative enterprises to poverty reduction, employment generation and social integration. The Year will also highlight the strengths of the cooperative business model as an alternative means of doing business and furthering socioeconomic development. Membership in co-operative businesses has grown to 1 billion people across 96 countries. In 2008, the world's 300 largest co-ops generated revenues of more than US$1.6 trillion.[52]

The nation of Spain is the home of two impressive cooperatives, one industrial and one agricultural. The *industrial cooperative* is Mondragon a corporation and federation of worker cooperatives based in the Basque region. The Mondragon Cooperative Corporation (MCC) started with a small stove manufacturing shop in 1956. Based on its success, additional cooperatives in a variety of manufacturing, agricultural, and service businesses were added and flourished. The MCC is now a multi-billion dollar complex of linked worker/member-owned business, service, and education enterprises employing over 30,000 people. Mondragon proved that cooperative ownership and management is a viable alternative economic system to capitalism, even in the context of high technology manufacturing and international trade, at which MCC excels.[53]

The Mondragon model has great potential. In 2009 the United Steel Workers signed an agreement with the Mondragon Corporation to collaborate in establishing unionized cooperatives based on the Mondragon model in manufacturing here and in Canada. USW International President Leo W. Gerard said, "Too often we have seen Wall Street hollow out companies by draining their cash and assets and hollowing out communities by shedding jobs and shuttering plants. We need a new business model that invests in workers and communities."

Highlighting the differences between Employee Stock Ownership Plans (ESOPs) and union co-ops, Gerard said, "We have lots of experience with ESOPs, but have found that it doesn't take long for the Wall Street types to push workers aside and take back control. We see Mondragon's cooperative model with 'one worker, one vote' ownership as a means to re-empower workers and make business accountable to Main Street instead of Wall Street."[54]

The *agricultural cooperative* is found in the Province of Almeria in southeast Spain. In the 1950's and 1960's this area was known for its abject poverty and barren land. It is now the top fruit and vegetable growing province in Spain and the largest cooperative vegetable growing area in Europe. The sector provides direct employment to more than 40,000 workers annually. More than 250 complementary or auxiliary businesses, both cooperatives and investor owned have been created with an annual turnover of more than 1,000 million Euros.[55]

Incorporating Cooperative Values in the Corporate Mode

While there is a general impression that corporations are large impersonal private organizations run for their own profits and without regard to wider interests, that is not always the case. There are still individual or family-run corporations that care deeply for the welfare of their workers, provide health care and retirement benefits to the best of their financial ability and are good citizens in their community and sensitive to the environment in which they function.

Regrettably, many of these small corporations have been squeezed out of the market by big box stores or sold to large national or international corporations, listed on stock exchanges where the main criteria is the profits on the bottom line and the most recent quarterly financial report.

One of the best sources for finding **corporations with a conscience** is in the list of companies held by socially responsible mutual funds. PAX World Fund, started by Methodist Church activists in the Washington, D.C. area was one of the early socially responsible mutual funds. Calvert and Domini soon followed and today there are dozens. Each has its own screen for companies they include in their definition of socially responsible corporations. They often screen for workers' rights, human rights, environment, weapons, nuclear power, community involvement, management policies, alcohol, tobacco and gambling. Some are active in taking proxies to shareholder meetings and urging better corporate policies.

"B" corporations

In certain states, companies can register as "B Corporations" (B Corp) where the "B" stands for benefit. B Corp registration allows a company to subordinate profits to social and environmental goals. Without this legal authorization, stockholders could in theory sue a CEO if profit making is not his sole objective. This was reported to be the reason that Ben and Jerry's sold their popular ice cream enterprise to a multinational conglomerate when they might have wished to do otherwise. B-Corp status ensures that specific goals can be met by different companies (manufacturers have different requirements from retail stores). It also helps with social marketing and branding. Thus, King Arthur Flour, which is a highly successful employee-owned business in Vermont, can be explicit, stating that "making money in itself is not our highest priority." Several states including California, Maryland, New Jersey, New York, Vermont, Virginia and Hawaii have passed legislation that permits B Corp chartering. Legislation is currently pending in North Carolina, Pennsylvania, Michigan, Colorado, and the District of Columbia.[56]

A separate nonprofit entity "B Lab" that is often confused with B corporations does research on a corporation's policies and issues a "Certified B Corporation" label if it meets their standards. According to their website, "there are over 450 Certified B Corporations across 60 different industries. From food and apparel to attorneys and office supplies, B Corporations are a diverse community with one unifying goal: to redefine success in business."[57]

Worker-owned Corporations

There are more than 11,000 companies owned entirely or in significant part by some 13.6 million employees. Most have adopted Employee Stock Ownership Plans (ESOPs). ESOPs democratize ownership, though only some of them involve participatory management. W.L. Gore, maker of Gore-Tex and many other products, is a leading example: the company has some 9,000 employee-owners at forty-five locations worldwide and generates annual sales of $2.5 billion. Litecontrol, which manufactures high-efficiency, high-performance architectural lighting fixtures, operates as a less typical ESOP; the Massachusetts-based company is entirely owned by roughly 200 employees and fully unionized with the International Brotherhood of Electrical Workers.

A different large-scale corporation, Seventh Generation—the nation's leader in "green" detergents, dishwashing soap, baby wipes, tissues, paper towels and other household products—has internal policies requiring that no one be paid more than fourteen times the lowest base pay or five times higher than the average employee.[58]

The Commons

Peter Barnes, the founder of Working Assets, has made a mind-stretching proposal to declare the sky and other aspects of nature to be a part of the commons owned by all of us and held in trust for present and future generations. He proposes that corporations should pay for their use/misuse of the commons; the payments would then be distributed equally to all of us, the owners of the commons—to go for retirement, education or other purposes we might choose. The Alaska Permanent Fund, as he notes, has already set the precedent by paying equal annual dividends to all Alaskans based on income from state oil leases.[59]

What is the Economy for? A New Answer

Cooperative business enterprise provides a new answer to the question—what is the economy for?

Whether small or large scale, a cooperative is owned and managed by its members for the mutual benefit of all members and their communities. Stability, security, and community are the goals of the cooperative economy.

As previously noted, Credit Unions (financial cooperatives) did not suffer the damage many banks brought on themselves in the financial collapse of 2008-2009. Credit Unions are not structured or motivated by the forces that caused much of the banking industry to engage in the high-risk, profit-seeking behavior that led to the collapse. They kept to the values of stability, security, and community.

Cooperatives, worker-owned shops, B corporations, and public trust institutions all prove that the economy can be run, and run better, by making good livelihoods and strong communities the reason for business enterprise.

Boundless Bull

Herman E. Daly

Herman Daly is a founding figure in the field of Ecological Economics. This article[60] was written in 1990 when the bubble of the growth economy was beginning to peak and mainstream economists considered a collapse, such as the one of 2008-2009, impossible. It remains a classic statement on the growth dynamic that government and business consider normative and are now working to restore. Daly lays out the critical impasse that confronts the unlimited growth economy.

If you want to know what is wrong with the American economy, it is not enough to go to graduate school, read books, and study statistical trends, you also have to watch TV. Not the talking-head shows or even documentaries, and especially not the network news, but the really serious stuff—the commercials. For instance, the most penetrating insight into the American economy by far is contained in the image of the bull that trots unimpeded through the countless Merrill Lynch commercials.

One such ad opens with a bull trotting along a beach. He is a very powerful animal—nothing is likely to stop him. And since the beach is empty as far as the eye can see, there is nothing that could even slow him down. A chorus in the background intones: "to … know … no … boundaries …" The bull trots off into the sunset.

Abruptly the scene shifts. The bull is now trotting across a bridge that spans a deep gorge. There are no bicycles, cars, or eighteen-wheel trucks on the bridge, so again the bull is alone in an empty and unobstructed world. An empty bridge conveniently spans the chasm, which might have proved a barrier to the bull, which after all is not a mountain goat.

Next, the bull finds himself in a forest of giant redwoods, looking just a bit lost as he tramples the underbrush. The camera zooms up the trunk of a giant redwood whose top disappears into the shimmering sun. The chorus chirps on about a "world with no boundaries."

Finally, we see the bull silhouetted against a burgundy sunset, standing in solitary majesty atop a mesa overlooking a great empty southwestern desert. The silhouette clearly outlines the animal's genitalia; making it obvious even to city slickers that this is a bull, not a cow. Fadeout. The bull cult of ancient Crete and Indus Valley, in which the bull god symbolized the virile principle of generation and invincible force, is alive and well on Wall Street.

The message is clear: Merrill Lynch wants to put you into an individualistic, macho world without limits—the U.S. economy. The bull, of course also symbolizes rising stock prices and unlimited optimism, which is ultimately based on this vision of an empty world where strong, solitary individuals have free reign. This vision is what is most fundamentally wrong with the American economy. In addition to TV commercials it can be found in politician's speeches, in economic textbooks, and between the ears of most economists and business journalists.

No bigger lie can be imagined. The world is not empty; it is full! Even where it is empty of people it is full of other things. In California it is so full of people they shoot each other because freeway space is scarce. A few years ago they were shooting each other because gasoline was scarce. Reducing the gasoline shortage just aggravated the space shortage on the freeways.

Many species are driven to extinction each year due to takeover of their "empty" space habitat. Indigenous peoples are relocated to make way for dams and highways through "empty" jungles. The "empty" atmosphere is dangerously full of carbon dioxide and pollutants that fall as acid rain.

Unlike Merrill Lynch's bull, most do not trot freely along empty beaches. Most are castrated and live their short lives as steers imprisoned in crowded, stinking feedlots. Like steers, we too live in a world of imploding fullness. The bonds of community, both moral and biophysical, are stretched, or rather compressed, to the breaking point. We have a massive foreign trade deficit, a domestic federal deficit, unemployment, declining real wages, and inflation. Large accumulated debt, both foreign and domestic are being used to finance consumption, not investment. Foreign ownership of the U.S. economy is increasing, and soon domestic control over national economic life will decrease.

Why does Merrill Lynch—and other media and academia and politicians—regale us with this "boundless bull?" Do they believe it? Why do they want you to believe it, or at least to be influenced by it at a subconscious level? Because what they are selling is growth, and growth requires empty space to grow into. Solitary bulls don't have to share the world with other creatures, and neither do you! Growth means that what you get from your bullish investments does not come at anyone else's expense. In a world with no boundaries, the poor can get richer while the rich get richer even faster. Our politicians find the boundless bull cult irresistible.

The boundless bull of unlimited growth appears in economics textbooks with less colorful imagery but greater precision. Economists abstract from natural resources because they do not consider them scarce, or because they think they can be perfectly substituted by man-made capital. The natural world either puts no obstacles in the bull's path, or, if an obstacle like the chasm appears, capital—the bridge—effectively removes it.

Economics textbooks also assume that wants are unlimited. Merrill Lynch's boundless bull is always on the move. What if, like Ferdinand,[61] he was to just sit, smell the flowers, and be content with the world as it is without trampling it underfoot? That would not do. If you were selling continual growth then you have to sell continual, restless, trotting dissatisfaction with the world as it is, as well as the notion that it has no boundaries.

The pre-analytic vision colors the analysis even of good economists, and many people never get beyond the boundless bull scenario. Certainly the media have not. Would it be asking too much of the media to do what professional economists have failed to do? Probably so, but all disciplines badly need external critics, and in the universities, disciplines do not criticize each other. Even philosophy, which historically was the critic of the separate disciplines, has abdicated that role.

Who is left? Economist Joan Robinson put it well many years ago when she noted that economists have run off to hide in thickets of algebra and left the serious problems of economic policy to be handled by journalists. Is it to the media that we must turn for disciplinary criticism, for new analytic thinking about the economy? The thought does not inspire confidence. But "in the land of the blind, the one-eyed man is king." If journalists are to criticize the disciplinary orthodoxy of economic growth, they will need both the energy provided by moral outrage and the clarity of thought provided by some basic analytic distinctions.

Moral outrage should result from the dawning realization that we are destroying the capacity of the earth to support life and counting it as progress, or at best as the inevitable cost of progress. "Progress" evidently means converting as much as possible of creation into our furniture and ourselves. "Ourselves" means, concretely, the unjust combination of overpopulated slums and over-consuming suburbs. Since we do not have the courage to face up to sharing and population control as the solution to injustice, we pretend that further growth will make the poor better off instead of simply making the rich richer. The wholesale extinctions of other species, and some primitive cultures within our own species, are not reckoned as costs. The intrinsic value of other species, their own capacity to enjoy life, is not admitted at all in economics, and their instrumental value as providers of ecological life-support services to humans is only dimly perceived. Costs and benefits to future humans are routinely discounted at 10 percent, meaning that each dollar of cost or benefit fifty years in the future is valued at less than a penny today.

But just getting angry is not sufficient. Doing something requires clear thinking, and clear thinking requires calling different things by different names. The most important analytic distinction comes straight from the definitions of growth and development. "Growth" means a quantitative increase in the scale of the physical dimensions of the economy. "Development" means the qualitative improvement in the structure, design and composition of the physical stocks of wealth that results from greater knowledge, both of technique and of purpose. A growing economy is getting larger. An economy can therefore develop without growing, or grow without developing. A steady-state economy is one that does not grow, but is free to develop. It is not static. Births replace deaths and production replaces depreciation so that stocks of wealth and people are continually renewed and improved, although neither is growing. Consider a steady-state library. Its stock of books is constant but not static. As a book becomes worn out or obsolete it is replaced by a new or better one. The quality of the library improves, but its physical stock of books does not grow. The library develops without growing. Likewise the economy's physical stock of people and artifacts can develop without growing.

The advantage of defining growth in terms of change in physical scale of the economy is that it forces us to think about the effects of a change in scale and directs attention to the concepts of an ecologically sustainable scale, or perhaps even of an optimal scale. The scale of the economy is the product of population times per capita resources use, i.e., the total flow of resources, a flow that might conceivably be ecologically unsustainable, especially in a finite world that is not empty.

The notion of an optimal scale for an activity is the very heart of microeconomics. For every activity, be it eating ice cream or making shoes, there is a cost function and a benefit function, and the rule is to increase the scale of the activity up to the point where rising marginal cost equals falling marginal benefit, i.e., to where the desire for another ice cream is equal to the desire to keep the money for something else, or the extra cost of making another pair of shoes is just equal to the extra revenue from selling the shoes. Yet for the macro level, the aggregate of all microeconomic activities (shoe making, ice cream eating, and everything else), there is no concept of optimal scale.

The notion that the macroeconomy could become too large relative to the ecosystem is simply absent from macroeconomic theory. The macroeconomy is supposed to grow forever. Since Gross National Product adds costs and benefits together instead of comparing them at the margin, we have no macro level accounting by which an optimal scale could be identified. Beyond a certain scale, growth begins to destroy more values than it creates—economic growth gives way to an era of un-economic growth. But GNP keeps rising, giving us no clue as to whether we have passed that critical point!

The apt image for the U.S. economy, then, is not the boundless bull on the empty beach, but the proverbial bull in the china shop. The boundless bull is too big and clumsy relative to its delicate environment. Why must it keep growing when it is already destroying more than its extra mass is worth? Because:

We fail to distinguish growth from development, and we classify all scale expansion as "economic growth" without even recognizing the possibility of "un-economic growth," i.e., growth that costs more than it is worth at the margin.

We refuse to fight poverty by redistribution and sharing, or by controlling our own numbers, leaving "economic growth" as the only acceptable cure for poverty.

But once we are beyond the optimal scale, and growth makes us poorer rather than richer, even that reason becomes absurd. Sharing, population control, and true qualitative development are difficult. They are collective virtues that for the most part cannot be attained

85

by individual action and that do not easily give rise to increased opportunities for private profit. The boundless bull is much easier to sell, and profitable at least to some while the illusion lasts. But further growth has become destructive of community, the environment, and the common good. If the media could help economists and politicians to see that, or at least to entertain the possibility that such a thing might be true, they will have rendered a service far greater than all the reports of statistics on GNP growth, Dow Jones indexes, and junk bond prices from now until the end of time.

Facing the Growth Dilemma
Stephen Loughin

Introduction

When I was about three years old, I remember my father carrying me outside on a cold winter night on Cape Cod, and pointing overhead to a speck of light moving across the sky, and telling me about Sputnik, the Soviet satellite that launched the space race. Children's games changed from cowboys and Indians, to astronauts and aliens. The cultural message was clear: the frontier remains boundless, it's just moving from the Wild West and into outer space. When Apollo 11 finally reached the moon, the astronauts captured dramatic photographs of Earth as seen from the moon. People began to understand Earth as a spaceship, an idea proposed in 1965 by Kenneth Boulding,[62] and then popularized in 1969 by R. Buckminster Fuller.[63] Meanwhile, the cost of launching people and freight into space remained fairly steady at about $10,000 per pound, despite decades and billions spent on research. The dream of transferring our growth economy to the final frontier of space remains out of reach nearly 50 years later. It seems that we will have to stop playing cowboys and Indians, and learn to live, as good astronauts must, within the limits of our finite spaceship Earth. This essay will examine one of those limitations, the limits to economic growth and how Quaker testimonies and the ethic of right relationship can help us achieve a life that is rich in Spirit, and abundantly blessed within the limits of good stewardship.

Growth

We are familiar with growth through our own childhood development. We look forward to growing taller and stronger, as our minds and bodies gain new abilities. This growth has a natural limit, and tapers off as we reach our 20s. However, there is another kind of growth process that continues so long as there is sufficient energy to sustain it. This is geometric or exponential growth, in which the amount added is proportional to the amount already present. Such growth will occur in yeast cultures, so long as there is sufficient food and dissipation of waste products. In the first period, one yeast organism buds and becomes two, then four, then eight, and so on. If births exceed deaths the population will grow. Rates of growth are constant so long as conditions remain the same, but for humans, conditions have changed dramatically.

Using the United Nations' estimates of worldwide population,[64] there has been a remarkable decrease in the time needed to double the population, a consequence of agricultural and technological advances that favor survival and longevity. Between the end of the Roman Empire and the time of the First Crusade, world population grew hardly at all, increasing by only about three percent over the first millennium (CE). But with advances in agriculture at the end of the Middle Ages, the doubling time dropped to 1450 years. After a brief setback due to the Black Death in the 1400s, growth increased and the doubling time dropped further to 500 years. With the industrial revolution, the time between doublings fell markedly to just about 100 years at the beginning of the 20th century. Further improvements in basic healthcare now yield a doubling every 60 years. People now in their eighties are the first humans ever to witness a tripling of world population in a single lifetime, from two billion in 1930 to the nearly seven billion of the present day.[65]

While these population trends are alarming, they are compounded by the fact that the economic activity of these seven billion people is also growing exponentially, independent of the underlying population growth. That is to say, there are systemic factors that drive us to a growth economy even in countries where the population is relatively stable, as it is in much of the developed world. Between 1980 and 2009, the global gross domestic product increased by more than a factor of two, correcting for inflation. This is considerably faster than the 60-year doubling of the population itself. While this is partly due to economic explosions in Asia and South America, growth is baked-in to our present day economy by the fact that it is almost entirely based on debt.

Money

Traditional teaching about money is that it developed as a medium of exchange motivated by convenience. Rather than trying to exchange half of a cow for forty geese, we turned to exchanging tokens of value—tokens that could be divided into small enough units for little transactions, but sufficiently compact to be transported and to accommodate large transactions as well. The first currencies may have been beads or shells, then copper, silver, and gold coins; but the important fact about them was that they were difficult to fabricate independently. The bearer of a certain amount of currency could reasonably be assumed to have provided a certain amount of value to the economy in his or her past transactions in order to accumulate those tokens. This is a fundamental assumption about money, and the reason that counterfeiting has been dealt with so harshly over the years. If one is allowed to participate in the economy with falsely obtained or fabricated tokens, then the good faith of a value-for-value exchange is corrupted.

The practice of lending money is ancient, and Jesus both preached about it (*Luke* 6:34) and engaged in direct action against it (*Matthew* 21:12). Lending is encouraged in the Old Testament, but usury, the charging of interest, is forbidden (*Exodus* 22:25 and *Leviticus* 25:37). Yet lending at interest is the cornerstone of modern banking and indeed, the global monetary system itself. Prior to the 17th century, loans were made in actual coin, and while the money was in use by the borrower, it could not also be in use by the lender. Sometimes, such loans were made to a monarch, generally for the prosecution of war, and then, depending on the outcome, the loans were sometimes not repaid.

In 1694, the Bank of England was created to solve this problem.[66] Rather than lending gold and silver directly, the aristocracy could place their money on deposit at the bank, and the bank would lend it to the crown, to be repaid with interest. In return for their deposits, the lenders were given a bank note, certifying their deposit. These bank notes soon began to circulate as if they were the money itself. As the practice of using paper money gained acceptance, the gold and silver could stay in the bank, and both the government's soldiers and the aristocrats' merchants came to accept the paper money in lieu of actual coin. This meant that the same amount of money, in actual gold and silver, was now backing twice that amount in circulation. Moreover, one-half of that amount was to be repaid with interest. This was the birth of fractional reserve banking and the original reserve ratio was 50 percent, which is to say that gold and silver deposits were backing 50 percent of the paper in circulation. At the time, only a small portion of the total money supply was circulating as paper currency, and while some of the coin in circulation was also borrowed money, the overall economic load of the interest was still relatively small.

Over the years, bankers have worked to decrease the reserve requirement to less than 10 percent, which means that more than 90 percent of the money in circulation is borrowed at interest, and less than 10 percent represents depositors' funds. Moreover, the legal ties between currency and precious metals, like gold and silver, have been broken, and so today's money is a ***fiat currency*** with no intrinsic value. Bankers essentially create money every time they make a loan, and in the U.S. they are allowed by law to lend $9 for every $1 they hold in reserve. Unfortunately, this is precisely the situation described earlier, in which some are allowed to participate in the economy with fabricated tokens, and even though this is perfectly legal, the fundamental good faith of a fair, value-for-value exchange is broken.

Consequence

The wholesale adoption of fractional reserve banking by banks throughout the world has had several disturbing consequences. One is that there has been a global explosion of debt. According to the CIA, the total public and private debt globally in 2009 was just under $57 trillion, which is about the same as the global gross domestic product. Even if private debt is excluded, government debt is equal to about 56 percent of global GDP. All of this debt, public and private, is earning interest. But how is all this interest to be paid?

One way of dealing with excessive public indebtedness is to *monetize* the debt, essentially debasing (alloying) the coin or printing paper money to pay back the creditors. Historically, this has resulted in hyperinflation because there is a large increase in the money supply, without a matching increase in the supply of goods and services. Most of the world's governments are no longer at liberty to do this, as their debts are often in the form of *sovereign bonds,* which are denominated in a foreign currency. Even the U.S. has to observe restraints, in that the recent quantitative easing, proposed by the Federal Reserve, is targeted to inflate the currency by only three percent.

The other alternative is to become more productive. In an earlier age, growing the population and settling more of the frontier, thereby increasing the size and scope of the nation's economic output, accomplished this. As the frontier closes, the only other alternative is to improve technology and reduce costs—often by outsourcing—to achieve higher production at lower expense. Unfortunately, this increased production is pointless if there is insufficient demand for the additional product. This is why there is such emphasis on consumer marketing today.

Yet another consequence of this indebtedness is that it has tilted the economic *production function*—the combination of capital, labor, land and resources needed to make a product—so that nearly all of the rewards now go to capital. Labor and the other factors have become commodities to be sourced by the lowest bidder in a global competition for the table scraps of the world economy. Symptoms of this are the increasing disparity between rich and poor, and the rampant unemployment and underemployment of both skilled and unskilled workers in all but the lowest-wage markets.

Like alcoholics, we first need to recognize that our over-consumption and our private and public indebtedness is an addiction. We have to want to break the cycle of borrowing, spending, consuming, and wasting what God has entrusted to us. Annie Leonard remarks that 90 percent of consumer purchases end up on the trash heap within 6 months. We must learn to be good stewards and live within not only our economic means, but our ecological niche as well. Our consumerism is harming the planet: melting the ice caps, extinguishing species, and infringing on our own health and well-being, or at least that of our poorer neighbors. Changing this will not be easy. The current economic system has been hundreds of years in the making and those who profit from it will not simply walk away from their game without an argument.

Quaker Testimonies

Fortunately, the wisdom of Quaker testimonies can serve as a guidepost to dealing with this dilemma. The testimonies point the way toward a fulfilling, spirit-led life of abundant sufficiency that can liberate us from the growth dilemma. Yet here are several ways in which our testimonies are in direct conflict with the world today.

We believe in equality, but economic inequality has increased dramatically, both nationally and internationally. Moreover, it is the world's poor who bear the brunt of environmental damage caused by consumerism.

We strive for integrity, yet the Gross Domestic Product (GDP), which drives our policies, is a false measure of prosperity. GDP includes spending on war, and on waste and destruction we ourselves create. To be truthful, our measures should reflect all social and environmental costs, including costs to future generations of our uses and abuses of earth's resources.

We turn toward simplicity, while our "growth economy" depends on ever-increasing consumption, fueled by debt, and damaging the fragile ecosystem on which our lives depend.

We value community, however, the number of people without secure employment, without health insurance, and confined to prisons is increasing, while our communities and the commonwealth of life, created by God, are steadily diminished by materialism.

We work for peace, but worldwide strife and devastation are the direct result of our dependence on fossil fuels. John Woolman urged Friends to "try" their possessions to see whether they "nourished the seeds of war." We must now ask the same question of our energy-intensive life-styles. Is God really calling us to *dominion* and its concomitant aggrandizement of living standards, or to *stewardship* and ecologically sound adaptation to Earth's ecosystems?

Call to Action

We need to begin a process of discernment about how we are led to respond to this concern. A movement is gathering, in which we begin to walk more gently over the earth. While many of us are becoming more aware of the little things we can do in our own lives to live simply and in a more Earth-friendly way, these are not, by themselves, enough to save the planet or solve the economic problem. We also need to become involved as families, churches and meetings, civic groups, and local communities in taking direct and non-violent action to change both local practices and societal institutions of economy and governance. Some of this is straightforward, though perhaps not easy.

Begin with *simplicity*: John Woolman recognized that when we live more simply, we have more time for attending to, what he called, "our inner Guide," and have more resources to devote to God's work. Debt is a complication in life, and getting out of debt, especially consumer debt, is a good first step toward simplification of life. Wealth can also be a kind of entanglement. Moving surplus wealth into activities that advance social and environmental integrity, while still complicated, does place wealth management into a straightforward focus on basic values, the ethic of right relationship. A new movement around money is rapidly developing. Its slogan is "move your money," which calls for personally and organizationally "defunding" the mega-banks and transferring the assets we control to local credit unions and thrift institutions where lending is less likely to support global financial speculation and more likely to support the community.

We can examine our consumption patterns. Economists tell us that we are rational consumers, each one maximizing our own utility and minimizing our costs. But if anything, we have been irrational consumers. Do we really need what we buy? Is it made to last? Is it made in a way that minimizes damage to the environment? Is it fixable and recyclable? Is it made by people who were paid fairly for their efforts? We have been encouraged and conditioned to act as though the advertised sticker price is the full cost of owning a thing, but we know, or can easily find out through a little examination and reflection, that it is not. The lack of full-cost accounting in the economic system has been called "the great evasion" of our time.

We can work to build our communities. The relentless pursuit of economic growth has torn the fabric of our society. The maximization of profit and minimization of cost have left whole segments of our society adrift without rudder or sail. What skills do we have in comparison to those our grandparents and great-grandparents had? So many of us now specialize, whereas our ancestors were successful precisely because they were generalists. We can rebuild our skill sets, and encourage diversity of skills in our community by teaching what we know. We can hire local talent when something needs to be done. Get to know who does what, and help other people make connections. Plant a garden. Share what we grow. Join a cooperative or support community agriculture. We are still villagers at heart. Urban environments are being renewed by the reemergence of the "village" ethos and neighborhood associations.

Early Quakers had an intriguing expression of greeting when they met up with another Friend. They often asked, "How fares the Truth with thee?" This was, and is, a shorthand way of keeping engagement with Quaker testimonies and the integrity of right relationship at the forefront of consciousness and social encounter. Consider how the cause of justice, peace, and the integrity of Creation might be advanced if that were the first concern of everyone. We can speak out for justice and the well-being of life's commonwealth in our communities, our nations, and in the world. So much war and injustice is waged to protect the profitable interests of the wealthy. We can shine a light on these connections when we see them and work against public financing of such evil. Some may be called to civil disobedience or direct non-violent action in their witness. Others might be called to engage with the policy makers to effect change. All voices and talents are needed.

As a people, Quakers, along with other faith groups, need to begin serious stewardship of the spaceship on which God has placed us, and to also recognize that we aren't the only passengers. Policy changes, similar to those suggested by Herman Daly,[68] will move us toward the steward's role:

Forgive sovereign debt, or at least the interest on it. We must understand the burdensome yoke that sovereign debt has placed on the shoulders of the world's poor. Friends active in Haiti relief are aware that the abject poverty that nation endures to this day, is largely because of a reparation debt after the Slave Revolt of 1791-1804. This debt was so enormous it was not paid off until 1947! If their debt were forgiven, many nations would have resources to develop the necessary infrastructure and sustainable energy resources.

Educate women. Work toward, or fund the education of women in the developing nations. This is likely the most effective way to limit the growth in population.

Encourage a shorter work week and job sharing. Ask policy and business leaders to consider a shorter work week and job sharing. This will do much to distribute employment opportunities more equitably so that those able to work can find meaningful employment.

Question the fractional reserve banking system. Over 90 percent of the money in circulation is debt that requires interest payments. This is now an enormous burden on society at every level. What rule says that money must be created from debt? Perhaps a gradual and controlled monetization of the debt, with a concomitant increase in reserve requirements, is in order. While this will cause inflation, it can be controlled by adjusting the reserve requirement and might be considered an alternative "tax." This could be a progressive tax since it would tend to diminish the value of hoarded wealth. Wage earners, and even social security and welfare recipients, will see their incomes eventually adjusted to cover the loss in currency value. The threat of inflation can drive wealthy investors toward investments with higher risk, but higher potential reward, which can also be good for employment.

Work on monetary system reform. The work underway is gaining credibility as economic behavior must shift from a history of dominion and aggrandizement to stewardship and sufficiency. Huber and Robertson are mainstream veterans of the economic management, public policy, and civic governance professions working on why monetary reform is now critically necessary, and on how it can be accomplished.[69] Their analysis forms the background to the proposed

Bank of England (Creation of Currency) Bill 2011.[70] Representative Dennis Kucinich has introduced the National Emergency Employment Defense (NEED) Act of 2011, HR 2990 for monetary reform in the U.S. House of Representatives.[71]

We are beyond the point where our spaceship can be turned away from collision between our economic misbehavior in the past and the ecological damage in the present and future. But we are, perhaps, in a position to make it a glancing blow rather than a head-on impact. Quakers, along with many others who have grasped this essential dilemma of our ecological situation, can be the "trim-tabs"[72] that Buckminster Fuller talked about; working to counteract the turbulence as the world finally recognizes and begins to confront the growth dilemma.

Endnotes

(Full bibliographic citations below in Bibliography)

1   Brown and Garver (2009)

2   Ciscel (2007)

3   Dreby (2007)

4   Clarke (1987)

5   Helmuth (2011)

6   Peare (1956), Reps (1956), Lingelbach (1944)

7   Woolman (Moulton, 1971)

8   Woolman (Scudder, 1936)

9   Woolman (Olmstead (1987)

10 Document available from Keith Helmuth <ekhelmuth@mindspring. com>

11 Document available from Keith Helmuth <ekhelmuth@mindspring. com>

12 Mitchell (1967), Helmuth (1991)

13 Hinshaw (2006), Kates and Burton (1986)

14 Watson (1979, 1991)

15 Franklin (2006)

16 Franklin (1999)

17 Boulding (1956, 1988)

18 Boulding (1965)

19 Boulding (1966)

20 Friends Committee on National Legislation <FCNL.org>

21 Document available from Keith Helmuth <ekhelmuth@mindspring. com>

22 Levering (1999). Friends Committee on National Legislation (2004)

23 Quaker Earthcare Witness <quakerearthcare.org>

24 Document available from Keith Helmuth <ekhelmuth@mindspring. com>

25 American Friends Service Committee <afsc.org/sites/afsc.civicactions. net/files/documents/Dynamics of the Global Economy.pdf>

26 *Quaker Eco-Bulletin* 3:6 <quakerearthcare.org/Publications/ QuakerEcoBulletin/QEBArchive/QEB-PDF/QEB3-6-PendleHillLetter. pdf>

27 Quaker Institute for the Future <quakerinstitute.org>

28 Brown and Garver (2009)

29 Document available from Keith Helmuth <ekhelmuth@mindspring. com>

30 The Kabarak Call for Peace and Ecojustice <saltandlight2012.org/ kabarak-call-peace-and-ecojustice>

31 Smith (1776)

32 George (2001)

33 Robbins (1932)

34 Hicks (1953)

35 Galtung (1969)

36 Everest (1991)

37 James (2001)

38 Brown (2008), Balzli and Hornig (2008) Food & Water Watch (2009)

39 Woolman (1971 (Moulton, Ed.)

40 <independentwatertesting.com/education-center/148-what-is-the-halliburton-loophole.html>

41 Legal Services of New Jersey (2007)

42 McGurty (2007)

43 Bullard (2005) Bullard *et al* (2007, 2011)

44 Lakey (2011)

45 Concrete economic tools Norway used to move toward equality are available for the asking <glakey1@swarthmore.edu>

46 Washingtons Blog, November 9th, 2011 <ritholtz.com/blog/2011/11/ key-lesson-from-iceland-crisis-%E2%80%9Clet-banks-fail%E2%80%9D/>

47 Hill (2011)

48 *Philadelphia Yearly Meeting Faith and Practice*, 1961, page 41

49 *The Book of Discipline*, Baltimore Yearly Meeting, 1962, page 48

50 *Book of Discipline*, New York Yearly Meeting, 1950, page 54

51 University of Wisconsin Center for Cooperatives <reic.uwcc.wisc.edu>

52 International Year of Cooperatives <social.un.org/coopsyear>; World Watch Institute, Vital Signs: Global Trends that Shape our Future <vi-talsigns.worldwatch.org>

53 MacLeod (1997)

54 USW International President Leo W. Gerard in USW Press Release

dated October 27, 2009

55 Giagnocavo (2012)

56 Benefit Corp Information Center, State by State Legislative Status <benefitcorp.net/state-by-state-legislative-status>

57 Certified B Corp <bcorporation.net>

58 Alperovitz (2012)

59 Barnes (2001, 2006)

60 Daly (1990) Originally published in the *Gannett Center Journal for Media Studies*, Ithaca College, Summer Issue, 1990, this article is used with the author's permission.

61 Leaf (1936)

62 Boulding (1965)

63 Fuller (1969)

64 Population Division of the Department of Economic and Social Affairs of the United Nations Secretariat, World Population Prospects: The 2008 Revision, 28 Dec 2010, <esa.un.org/unpp>

65 Kunzig (2011)

66 Bank of England Act of 1694, established by Royal Charter of William & Mary, sealed 27th July 1694. <bankofengland.co.uk/about/history>

67 Leonard (2010)

68 Daly (2008)

69 Huber and Robertson (2001)

70 Bank of England (Creation of Currency) Bill 2011 <positivemoney. org.uk/wp-content/uploads/2012/02/Bank-of-England-Creation-of-Currency-Bill-Smaller.pdf>

71 Kucinich Bill <monetary.org/wp-content/uploads/2011/11/HR-2990. pdf>

72 Trim tabs are small surfaces connected to the trailing edge of a larger control surface on a boat or aircraft, used to control the trim of the controls, i.e. to counteract hydro- or aero-dynamic forces and stabilize the boat or aircraft in a particular desired attitude without the need for the operator to constantly apply a control force.

Bibliography

Alperovitz, Gar, The New-Economy Movement. *The Nation*, June 13, 2012 <thenation.com/article/160949/new-economy-movement>.

Balzli, Beat and Frank Hornig, 2008. Deadly Greed The Role of Speculators in the Global Food Crisis. *Speigel Online International* (04/23/2008) <spiegel.de/international/world/0,1518,549187,00.html>.

Barnes, Peter, 2001. *Who Owns the Sky? Our Common Assets and the Future of Capitalism.* Washington DC: Island Press.

Barnes, Peter, 2006. *Capitalism 3.0: A Guide to Reclaiming the Commons.* San Francisco: Berrett-Koehler

Boulding, Kenneth, 1956. *The Image: Knowledge in Life and Society.* Ann Arbor MI: University of Michigan Press.

Boulding, Kenneth E., 1965 *Earth as a Spaceship,* an Essay for the Committee on Space Sciences, Washington State University. 10 May 1965. Archives (Box #38) Colorado State University <colorado.edu/econ/Kenneth.Boulding/ spaceship-earth.html>.

Boulding, Kenneth, 1966. The Economics of the Coming Spaceship Earth. *Environmental Quality in a Growing Economy,* H. Jarrett, Ed. Washington, D.C.: RFF Press.

Boulding, Kenneth, 1988. *The Meaning of the 20th Century: The Great Transition.* Lanham MD: University Press of America.

Brown, Ellen, 2008. *Speculating In Hunger: Are Investors Contributing to the Global Food Crisis?* <webofdebt.com/articles/derivative-disaster. php >

Brown, Peter G., Geoffrey Garver, Keith Helmuth, Robert Howell and Steve Szeghi, 2009. *Right Relationship: Building a Whole Earth Economy,* San Francisco: Berrett-Kohler.

Bullard, Robert D., 2005. *The Quest for Environmental Justice: Human Rights and the Politics of Pollution.* San Francisco: Sierra Club Books.

Bullard, Robert D., Paul Mohai, Robin Saha, and Beverly Wright, 2007. *Toxic Wastes and Race at Twenty 1987-2007.* United Church of Christ Justice and Witness Ministries <ucc.org/assets/pdfs/toxic20.pdf>.

Bullard, Robert D., Glenn S. Johnson, Angel O. Torres, 2011. *Environmental Health and Racial Equity: Building Environmentally Just, Sustainable, and Livable Communities.*

Catton, William R., 1982. Overshoot: The Ecological Basis of Revolutionary Change. Urbana IL: University of Illinois Press.

Ciscel, David, 2007. It's the Economy, Friend. *Quaker Eco-Bulletin* 7:4.

Clarke, George, 1987. *John Bellers: His Life, Times & Writings.* London: Routledge & Kegan Paul.

Coyle, Diane, 2011. *The Economics of Enough: How to Run the Economy As If the Future Matters.* Princeton NJ: Princeton University Press.

Daly, Herman E., 1990. Boundless Bull. *Gannett Center Journal for Media Studies,* Ithaca College, Summer Issue, 1990.

Daly, Herman E., 1991. *Steady-State Economics,* 2nd Ed. Washington: Island Press.

Daly, Herman E. and John B. Cobb, 1994. *For the Common Good: Redirecting the Economy Toward Community, the Environment, and a Sustainable Future,* 2nd Ed. Boston: Beacon Press.

Daly, Herman E., 1996. *Beyond Growth: The Economics of Sustainable Development.* Boston: Beacon Press.

Daly, Herman E. and Joshua Farley, 2003. *Ecological Economics: Principles and Applications.* Washington: Island Press.

Daly, Herman, 2008. "Towards a Steady-State Economy," an essay commissioned by the Sustainable Development Commission for their Redefining Prosperity effort to advise the U.K. government. <theoildrum.com/pdf/theoildrum_3941.pdf>

Dreby, Ed, 2007. *Seeds of Violence, Seeds of Hope.* <quakerearthcare.org/PDFs/Seeds_Vol_I.pdf>.

Everest, Larry, 1991. "The Selling of Peru." Woods Hole, MA: *ZMagazine.* <zmag.org/Zmag/articles/sept94 everest.htm>

Food & Water Watch, 2009. *Casino of Hunger: How Wall Street Spectulators Fueled the Global Food Crisis.* <foodandwaterwatch.org/reports/casino>.

Franklin, Ursula, 1999. *The Real World of Technology,* Second Edition. Toronto: House of Anasi Press from CBC Massey Lectures, 1989 <cbc.ca/ideas/massey-archives/1989/11/07/1989-massey-lectures-the-real-world-of-technology>

Franklin, Ursula, 2006. *The Ursula Franklin Reader: Pacifism as a Map.* Michelle Swenarchuk, Ed. Toronto: Between the Lines.

Friends Committee on National Legislation, 2004. *Background on the UN Convention on the Law of the Sea.* <fcnl.org/issues/ppdc/background_on_the_un_convention_on_the_law_of_the_sea/>.

Fuller, R. Buckminster, 1969. *Operating Manual for Spaceship Earth.* Carbondale: Southern Illinois University Press.

Galtung, Johan, 1969. Violence, Peace, and Peace Research. *Journal of Peace Research* 6 (3): 167-191.

George, David, 2001. *Preference Pollution: How Markets Create the Desires We Dislike.* Ann Arbor MI: University of Michigan Press.

Giagnocavo, Cynthia, 2012. *The Almería Agricultural Cooperative Model: creating successful economic and social communities.* United

Nations, Division for Social Policy and Development, Department of Economic and Social Affairs <social.un.org/coopsyear/documents/ AlmeriaPaperGiagnocavo.pdf>.

Gibson, William E., 2004. *Ecojustice—The Unfinished Journey.* Albany NY: State University of New York Press.

Gilding, Paul, 2011. *The Great Disruption: Why the Climate Crisis Will Bring on the End of Shopping and the Birth of a New World.* New York: Bloomsbury Press.

Hamilton, Clive, 2003. *Growth Fetish. Crows Nest,* Australia: Allen and Unwin.

Heinberg, Richard, 2011. *The End of Growth: Adapting to Our New Economic Reality.* Gabriola Island BC: New Society Publishers.

Helmuth, Keith, 1991. *The Evolution of Environmental Education: The Early Years of Friends World College, 1965-1970.* <quakerinstitute.org/ wp-content/uploads/2010/04/Evol-of-Environ-Ed-FWC-2.rtf>.

Helmuth, Keith, 2011. *The Evolutionary Potential of Quakerism Revisited: Kenneth Boulding and John Bellers.* Woodstock NB & Houlton ME: Chapel Street Editions <quaker.ca/Publications/Evolutionary_ Potential_of_Quakerism_Revisited.pdf>.

Hicks, John, 1953. *Value and Capital: An inquiry into some Fundamental Principles of Economic Theory.* Oxford UK: Clarendon Press.

Hill, Symon, 2011. *Quakers, Ethics and Capitalism.* Ekklesia: A New Way of Thinking <ekklesia.co.uk/node/14583>.

Hinshaw, Robert E., 2006. *Living with Nature's Extremes: The Life of Gilbert Fowler White.* Boulder CO: Johnson Books.

Hofrichter, Richard, 2002. *Toxic Struggles: The Theory and Practice of Environmental Justice.* Salt Lake City: University of Utah Press.

Huber, Joseph and James Robertson, 2011. *Creating New Money: A Monetary Reform for the Information Age.* London: New Economics Foundation. <neweconomics.org/publications/creating-new-money >

Jackson, Tim, 2009. *Prosperity Without Growth: Economics for a Finite Planet.* London: Earthscan.

James, Susan, Janice Johnson, Chitra Raghavan, Diana Woolis, 2001. *Structural Violence: The Invisible Violence in our Communities.* Presented at the 129th Annual Meeting at the American Public Health Association, Atlanta GA.

Kates, Robert W. and Ian Burton, 1986. *Geography, Resources, and Environment,* Vol. 1: Selected Writings of Gilbert F. White. Chicago: University of Chicago Press.

Kennedy, Margrit, 1995. *Interest and Inflation Free Money: Creating an Exchange Medium that Works for Everybody and Protects the Earth.*

Gabriola Island BC: New Society Publishers <margritkennedy.de/books.html>.

Kunzig, Robert, 2011. Population 7 Billion. National Geographic, 219 (1) January, 2011.

Lakey, George, 2011. *Powerful Beyond Measure: The Legacy of Quaker Leadership in the 21st Century.* 2011 William Penn Lecture, Philadelphia Yearly Meeting <quakerbooks.org>.

Leaf, Munro, 1936. *The Story of Ferdinand.* New York: Viking Press.

Legal Services of New Jersey, 2007. *Poverty in the City of Camden.* Poverty Benchmarks Project, Poverty Research Institute <lsnj.org/PDFs/budget/PovertyCityOfCamden041107.pdf>.

Leonard, Annie, 2010. *The Story of Stuff.* New York NY: Free Press (Simon & Schuster).

Levering, Ralph B. and Miriam L. Levering, 1999. *Citizen Action for Global Change: The Neptune Group and Law of the Sea (Syracuse Studies on Peace and Conflict Resolution).* Syracuse NY: Syracuse University Press.

Lingelbach, William E., 1944. William Penn and City Planning. *Pennsylvania Magazine of History and Biography* 68 (4): 398-418, Philadelphia: The Historical Society of Pennsylvania.

MacLeod, Greg, 1997. *From Mondragon to America: Experiments in Community Economic Development.* Sydney NS: University College of Cape Breton Press.

McGurty, Eileen, 2007. *Transforming Environmentalism: Warren County, PCBs, and the Origins of Environmental Justice.* New Brunswick, NJ: Rutgers University Press.

Mitchell, Morris, 1967. *World Education: Revolutionary Concept.* New York: Pageant Press.

Peare, Catherine Owens, 1956. *William Penn: A Biography.* Ann Arbor MI: University of Michigan Press.

Reps, John W., 1956. William Penn and the Planning of Philadelphia. *Town Planning Review* 27 (4): 27-39, Liverpool: University of Liverpool Press.

Robbins, Lionel, 1932. *Essays on the Nature and Significance of Economic Science.* London: Macmillan.

Sale, Peter F., 2011. *Our Dying Planet: An Ecologist's View of the Crisis We Face.* Berkeley CA: University of California Press.

Simms, Andrew, 2005. *Ecological Debt: The Health of the Planet and the Wealth of Nations.* London: Pluto Press.

Smith, Adam, 1776 *An Inquiry into the Nature and Causes of the Wealth of Nations,* London: Methuen and Company, Ltd., reprinted in 1904.

Watson, Elizabeth, 1979. *Guest of My Life.* Burnsville NC: Celo Press.

Watson, Elizabeth, 1991. *Healing Ourselves and Our Earth.* Burlington VT: Quaker Earthcare Witness.

Wilkinson, Richard and Kate Pickett, 2010. *The Spirit Level: Why Greater Equality Makes Societies Stronger.* New York: Bloomsbury Press.

Woolman, John, 1936. *The Journal of John Woolman and Other Writings* (Vida Scudder edition). London: J.M. Dent, *Everyman's Library.*

Woolman, John, 1971. *Journal and Major Essays of John Woolman.* Phillips Moulton, Ed. New York: Oxford University Press.

Woolman, John, 1987. *Conversations on the True Harmony of Mankind and How It May Be Promoted*, Sterling Olmsted, Ed. Philadelphia: Wider Quaker Fellowship.

Contributors

Kenneth Boulding was a professor of economics at several institutions, most notably University of Michigan and University of Colorado. He was a founding figure in the fields of Systems Analysis and Peace Research.

Herman Daly is Professor Emeritus of Economics at the University of Maryland. He was formerly an economist with the World Bank. He is one of the founders of Ecological Economics.

Ed Dreby is a retired social studies teacher and secondary school administrator. He is the project leader of the Growth Dilemma Project.

Keith Helmuth has been a small business entrepreneur and community development activist. He is the Secretary of the Board of Trustees of the Quaker Institute for the Future.

Leonard Joy is an economist who has had an extensive career in international development work, principally with UN programs, as well as a variety of academic appointments. He is a founding Board Member of Quaker Institute for the Future.

George Lakey is a Visiting Professor at the Lang Center for Civic and Social Responsibility, Swarthmore College (PA). He founded the non-violent education organization, Training for Change and consults regularly with civic and labor organizations on strategies for change. He is a member of the Earth Quaker Action Team.

Stephen Loughin teaches physics at St. Joseph's University (PA). He is also a consultant on waste minimization strategies for material suppliers and provides technology support to a reading and literacy company he helped start in 1998. He is a member of the Growth Dilemma Project.

Margaret Mansfield is a retired social studies teacher and a member of the General Committee of Friends Committee on National Legislation.

David Ross is professor of economics at Bryn Mawr College and an active participant in Friends Association for Higher Education.

Ed Snyder is Executive Secretary Emeritus of Friends Committee on National Legislation and serves on Friends Committee on Maine Public Policy.

Quaker Institute for the Future

Advancing a global future of inclusion, social justice, and ecological integrity through participatory research and discernment.

The Quaker Institute for the Future (QIF) seeks to generate systematic insight, knowledge, and wisdom that can inform public policy and enable us to treat all humans, all communities of life, and the whole Earth as manifestations of the Divine. QIF creates the opportunity for Quaker scholars and practitioners to apply the social and ecological intelligence of their disciplines within the context of Friends' testimonies and the Quaker traditions of truth seeking and public service.

The focus of the Institute's concerns include:

- Economic behavior that increasingly undermines the ecological processes on which life depends.

- The development of technologies and capabilities that hold us responsible for the future of humanity and the Earth.

- Structural violence and lethal conflict arising from the pressures of change, increasing inequity, concentrations of power and wealth, declining natural capital, and increasing militarism.

- The increasing separation of people into areas of poverty and wealth, and into social domains of aggrandizement and deprivation.

- The philosophy of individualism and its socially corrosive promotion as the principal means for the achievement of the common good.

- The complexity of global interdependence and its demands on governance systems and citizen's responsibilities.

- The convergence of ecological and economic breakdown into societal disintegration.

<quakerinstitute.org>